Grasping the changing world

As different societies merge into one global society and face the concomitant crises of identity, of purpose and interest, social anthropology urgently needs to bring its methodology up to date: new methods are needed to analyse, compare and understand different cultures across space and time.

Grasping the Changing World collects papers read at the second biennial EASA conference in Prague in 1992. The conference took place in an extraordinary 'postmodern' setting. With the fall of the communist regimes in Central and Eastern Europe old certainties and time-honoured concepts had become obsolete; at the same time, anthropology too was in upheaval, and long-established patterns of thought seemed inadequate to grasp the rapidly changing realities. These doubts and tensions are reflected in this collection.

The first half of *Grasping the Changing World* focuses on ways of conceptualising, modelling and perceiving the present, while the second half reassesses the theoretical strength or otherwise of social anthropology as a modern social science. Combining methodological rigour and originality, this collection will make invaluable reading for all students of social anthropology, sociology and politics.

Václav Hubinger is an adviser at the Czech Ministry of Foreign Affairs and Research Fellow at the Institute of Ethnography in Prague.

European Association of Social Anthropologists

The European Association of Social Anthropologists (EASA) was inaugurated in January 1989, in response to a widely felt need for a professional association which would represent social anthropologists in Europe, and foster co-operation and interchange in teaching and research. As Europe transforms itself in the 1990s, the EASA is dedicated to the renewal of the distinctive European tradition in social anthropology.

In the same series:

Grasping the changing world

Anthropological concepts in the postmodern era

Edited by Václav Hubinger

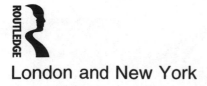

London and New York

First published 1996
by Routledge
11 New Fetter Lane, London EC4P 4EE

Simultaneously published in the USA and Canada
by Routledge
29 West 35th Street, New York, NY 10001

Routledge is an International Thomson Publishing company

© 1996 Václav Hubinger for selection and editorial matter, individual chapters
the contributors

Typeset in Times by LaserScript, Mitcham, Surrey
Printed and bound in Great Britain by
TJ Press Ltd, Padstow, Cornwall

British Library Cataloguing in Publication Data
A catalogue record for this book is available from the British Library

Library of Congress Cataloguing in Publication Data
A catalogue record for this book has been requested

ISBN 0–415–10201–4 (hbk)
ISBN 0–415–10202–2 (pbk)

Contents

Contributors

Olivia Harris, is Head of Department of Anthropology at Goldsmiths' College, University of London. She has conducted fieldwork in highland Bolivia on gender, the peasant economy, and more recently on oral history and ethnohistory. She is on the editorial board of several professional periodicals and has served as Vice-President of the Royal Anthropological Institute. She has published widely on gender, the household, Andean ethnography and conceptualisations of time and history.

Václav Hubinger is part-time Research Fellow at the Institute of Ethnology, Czech Academy of Sciences. He has published on both ethnicity and nation-building processes. His areas of interest comprise Southeast Asia, Central Europe and South Africa. He is currently carrying out research on the role of ethnography in creating Czech national awareness and nationalism. His publications include *The Creation of Indonesian National Identity* (Prague: UEF 1992) and *Zebra na zabití* ('Zebra to be Killed'; Prague, 1994).

Igor Krupnik is a Research Anthropologist at the Arctic Studies Center of the Smithsonian Institution in Washington, DC. Born and educated in Russia, he conducted fieldwork in various parts of the former Soviet Union, including Siberia, the Russian Arctic, and the Caucassus where he studied traditional social systems, subsistence and local ethnohistory. He is currently researching cultural preservation and modern changes among circumpolar peoples. His recent publications include *Arctic Adaptation: Native Whalers and Reindeer Herders in Northern Eurasia* (New England University Press, 1993). He is on the editorial board of both *Arctic Anthropology* and *Etudes/Inuit/Studies*, and is a council member of the International Arctic Social Science Association.

Carla Pasquinelli is Associated Professor at the Department of Social Sciences, Istituto Universitario Orientale, Naples. She has conducted fieldwork in Somalia and is the editor of *Parolechiave*. She is interested in the theory of anthropology and in power; rituals; ethnicity; and cultural change. Her publications include *Beyond the Culture of War* (Rome: Telos, 1985), *Fondamentalismi* (Rome: Parolechiave, 1994).

Tim Quinlan is a Research Officer at the Institute for Social and Economic Research, University of Durban-Westville, South Africa. He has conducted fieldwork in Lesotho and South Africa on land tenure and chieftainship. His recent research concentrates on topics related to environmental policy and planning. This work includes theoretical and methodological consideration of interdisciplinary research in southern Africa. His publications include 'South Africa's integrated environmental management policy' (1993).

C. W. Watson is Senior Lecturer in Anthropology at Eliot College, University of Kent at Canterbury. For several years he was head of the Centre of Southeast Asian Studies there. He has conducted extensive fieldwork in Malaysia and Indonesia. His main interests are modern history; Islam; ethnicity; literature; and autobiography. His publications include *Kerinci: Two Historical Studies* (University of Kent at Canterbury, 1984), *State and Society in Indonesia* (University of Kent at Canterbury, 1987) and *Understanding Witchcraft and Sorcery in Southeast Asia*, co-edited with R. Ellen (Honolulu: University of Hawaii Press, 1993).

Preface

This volume comprises papers from two panels of the Conference of the European Association of Social Anthropology (EASA) held in Prague in 1992. The panel convened by Václav Hubinger considered the topic 'The Making of the Past', and was concerned with the crucial role the past plays in the formation of the present. The panel convened by Peter Skalník, entitled 'Dealing with Unbounded Wholes', investigated the pressing need for the development of new concepts, or reconsideration of existing concepts to allow for analysis of a general notion of society rather than the study of individual societies considered as independent and self-contained units.

The outcome seemed to be that the specific concerns of each panel were basically the same: nation-building, tradition and culture; the differences lying only in the emphasis or angle taken by each panel. However, the initial plan was to publish the papers from each panel in separate volumes. This very quickly proved not to be the best approach, and a decision was taken to publish the papers in a single volume, a decision which has contributed to the considerable delay in the publication of these papers. The delay in publication has been fruitful in several respects.

Some of the papers read at the panel are missing from this volume: Valery A. Tishkov's contribution on ethnic conflicts and social science theory; Teresa del Valle has published her paper as part of her book *Korrika: Basque Ritual for Ethnic Identity* (Reno, Nev.: University of Nevada Press, 1993). The papers by Françoise Zonabend ('Anthropologie et modernité') and Peter Skalník ('Dealing with unbounded wholes') are also not included in this volume. Peter Skalník also decided to step down as co-editor due to his enormous workload. However, his contribution to the preparatory work has been important and I am very grateful to him for his assistance and friendly advice.

Quite naturally, neither of the panels exhausted the topic, nor did they converge completely as both addressed the world we live in – either by analysing its roots and the way it became our contemporary reality: or by investigating the way it exists as such. The term, or rather the concept, unbounded wholes is a suitable expression for capturing both the current state of this world and the movements within it. Old, past worlds became unbounded and so created the new or newly perceived world of today.

It does not seem necessary to introduce the volume with a chapter to explain and connect the elements of this collection. In my opinion, all the necessary connections are well expressed by their publication in a single volume, under a single title.

Václav Hubinger

Chapter 1

The temporalities of tradition
Reflections on a changing anthropology

Olivia Harris

'GRASPING THE CHANGING WORLD'

As tariff and political frontiers are eroded, and electronic technologies permit goods, information and money to move at the speed of a finger's touch on a computer key, it seems self-evident that anthropology is confronted by a substantial challenge to rethink its founding categories and redefine its projects. There is nothing new about change. None the less, it may well be true that a wholehearted grasping of change in its objects of study is relatively new for anthropology as a discipline! In the early stages of its history it privileged stability and continuity, and sought to classify and analyse races, customs, cultures and social structures which were treated as given entities. Even the evolutionary paradigm which was based on a theory of change conceived the pace of progress at such a slow rate that it could be observed in human populations only by comparing different stages as discrete entities.

There are many historical reasons why anthropology as it developed assumed that the groups and cultural traits it studied existed in a state of equilibrium or at least long-term stability. One is the nostalgia for an organic community that Robertson has suggested lay at the heart of the development of the social sciences (1990). Indeed in the emerging intellectual division of labour in the second half of the nineteenth century, it was the study of traditional cultures and groups that became the field of the developing ethnology/anthropology.[1] A further reason was that in the internal and external colonies where anthropologists so frequently worked, colonial administrations fixed social and political units which were previously fluid, and gradually codified the practices and values of subjugated peoples. Asad has recently suggested that, in this sense, anthropology is very much the child of colonialism, in that it took the codified version of local society as its model of reality (1991).

Furthermore, while there have been many intellectual and artistic currents that have embraced the implications of technological change and the compression of space and time (Kern 1983), the presuppositions of Cartesian and mechanistic philosophies, thoroughly ingrained in European intellectual traditions, have meant that a cosmology of change and transformation has been imbricated with a vision of the world as a stable object of contemplation, divided into distinct, identifiable 'things'.

It is a truism today to say that we live in an era of rapid and far-reaching change. The economic and technological infrastructure of this bias to constant change is obvious, and the cultural orientation to change equally well known. But how far is change an emic and how far an analytic category? How far does change as a concept depend on identifying a previous stable state as a necessary point of departure? In what circumstances might it be possible to argue that situations of permanent flux and transformation constitute in themselves a certain sort of stability?

These seem to me central issues for debate at a time when anthropology itself is also in a process of transformation. They concern our attempts to contribute to an understanding of the world in which we live, and at the same time they invite a reflexive consideration of the past and the historical development of our discipline. How far are anthropological concepts limited through being the product of the historical environment in which they first developed? Conversely, to what extent do the changes of lived history require changed or new concepts in the social sciences? What does change mean and how is it experienced?

Invoking the principle that we may gain insight into a phenomenon by looking at its antithesis, let us take the concept of tradition, which together with custom was for a long time considered to be the proper object of anthropological enquiry. The terms indicate notions of order, of legitimacy, and above all of continuity. They are closely allied semantically to the concept of genealogy, of linear descent from the past, in which something (the tradition, the custom) has been handed down to its present inheritors. The primary images invoked by the concept of tradition are those of a stable agrarian community in which kinship and collective values take precedence over the individual, using simple technology, with a strong oral culture and sense of the past, and bound by the rituals of production, nature and the personal life-cycle. Their power derives from the contrast with industrial production, urban living, the freedoms, the instability, the threat of anomie, the constant facing of new situations, the emphasis on individual autonomy. In this context, to discuss the concept of tradition is to interrogate the very category of change, and beyond that to ask about the possible forms in which a relationship with the past can be conceived and lived.

THE TEMPORALITIES OF TRADITION

The concept of tradition raises the question of how far present practices or cultural categories reveal an explicit link with the past. Anthropological approaches to this issue have altered radically over the decades. Although they are not necessarily couched directly or exclusively in terms of the concept of tradition, these changing approaches can perhaps best be identified by distinguishing three different 'moments', each of which is associated with a different temporality, a distinctive way of representing the relationship between past, present and future, and indeed of representing the present itself. It will be seen that these moments as I have distinguished them also correspond to a broader set of preoccupations and cultural movements. There are obvious historical implications in the labels I have selected; however they are not intended as a periodisation of the history of anthropology as such, rather as three different options as regards how tradition may be conceptualised, which have assumed greater salience at particular periods in different countries. For the sake of simplicity I shall refer to them respectively as modernist, structuralist and postmodernist.

The modernist moment

In temporal terms the modernist moment is constituted by the idea of rupture. The identification of the modern is first and foremost a question of temporality; the *Neuzeit* or *le moderne* was new with respect to what came before, thus registering a break with the past. Modernity is a category of historical periodisation defined solely in temporal terms, unlike for example mythic, religious or dynastic periodisations (Osborne 1992). The concept of modernity was also defined in terms of a new *quality* of temporality, intrinsically different from what had preceded it. It involved an exclusive valorisation of the present over the past in terms of the concepts of reason and progress. In Enlightenment thought reason was autonomous, able to validate its own laws to itself, within the present, without reference to the past or to tradition.

This temporal perspective is fundamental to the categories of Weberian sociology, and is still widely adhered to, for example, by Anthony Giddens, who asserts that modern social institutions are unique – distinct in form from all types of traditional order (e.g. 1990). If tradition is defined by means of the discourse of modernity, as has been so generally accepted in this century, the consequence is that it is treated mainly as a foil, as an other for the positive sign of modernity. For Giddens, as for Weber before him, tradition as a concept in itself is not a topic of much interest. It is more a discursive means for establishing and articulating an interest in the disenchanted and complex world which has increasingly been associated with the label of modernity.[2]

Another fundamental feature of the temporality of modernity is the temporal distancing that Johannes Fabian has so persuasively called 'allochrony' (Fabian 1983). Allochrony refers to the way in which populations that in chronological terms existed at the same time (i.e. they are synchronous) are assigned to different temporal periods usually seen in terms of evolutionary or historical progress (e.g. 'stone age' tribes of the twentieth century, or the 'ancient' way of life of peasants). The qualities of modernity – the now and the new – were identified unquestioningly with the European, and later American, centres so that, as a corollary, peripheral populations were seen as existing in some earlier temporal state. This contrasted 'other' time was spatialised so that tradition co-existed with modernity but in a different place. Nineteenth- and early-twentieth-century ethnology and anthropology were allochronic in this sense, and were premised on the absolute difference, expressed temporally, between those who studied and those who were studied.

Functionalist anthropology can be seen as a particularly modernist form of our discipline as Ardener has argued (1989). It was functionalism that most insistently identified the objects of anthropological investigation as stable and traditional and sought to theorise tradition on this basis.[3] It seems plausible to argue that the central place allotted to the study of kinship in anthropology is in part the consequence of this modernist temporality. Adam Kuper has argued that the 'invention of primitive society' by early anthropology required it to be the antithesis of the modern. Since the modern was associated with individualism and the separation of the public and private spheres, primitive society was by contrast identified with kinship (Kuper 1988). We can add that the images of tradition and continuity, which are so frequently invoked through the trope of genealogy, of descent, further overdetermine the centrality of kinship to the definition of traditional society. By contrast, a temporality of rupture places a negative value on enduring kinship lines and relationships.

However, not only functionalism was modernist in this temporal sense. So also was most ethnology and folklore studies whose object was defined as the other of modernity. Given this perspective, anthropology was often concerned with salvage, with shoring up the fragments broken apart by the coming of Europeans and colonialism, or, within the core areas of Europe, of the destructive impact of 'progress' and industrialisation. Nationalist anthropologies also fit here, in search of the authentic traditions from which nationalist movements and ethnic revitalisation must draw their inspiration, their symbolism. Indeed the past is a foundational resource in the search for a new collective identity, since modernity has been so associated with individuality and vice versa. This absolute contrast between the modern and the traditional coincides with that between individualism and community. Reason is above all the property of the autonomous individual, and the collective is considered an earlier, outmoded state.[4]

The impact of this constellation of ideas on anthropological thought remains strong. Theories of the 1930s, of 'social change' and 'culture contact' have given way to concepts of world system and globalisation, but the image of a definitive rupture with the past is as powerful as ever. At its inception, this image referred to an endogenous process within certain core areas of Europe, depicting a struggle between progressive reason and the dead hand of the past. However, if we look at the consequences of how this process of the break with past was exported to the rest of the world, the positive imagery is far harder to sustain. It usually involved a concerted assault on, and denial of, other peoples' pasts by exogenous colonising forces in the name of the projects of empire, progress, accumulation and religious conversion.

The structuralist moment

In contrast to the temporality of rupture typical of modernism, the structuralist moment is a temporality of continuity. The concept of tradition is not necessarily invoked directly, since it is closely associated with the discourse of modernity. None the less the approach which emphasises structure and continuity and minimises the significance of particular events has been of great importance to anthropological history. It seems to arise particularly out of the French intellectual tradition, which in a number of different ways has sought to minimise the premise of the 'great transformation' of modernity.[5] Simiand in 1903 denounced events as contingent and unintelligible. Later analyses of the meaning of the concept event make clear that it signifies a rupture or change, in contrast both to long-term evolution, and to those actions which reproduce the existing order (Sahlins 1991: 41, 45). Durkheim's dismissal of particular events as superficial manifestations of the deeper underlying processes was symptomatic of his broader concern with structure.[6] The fact that structure is in large part an architectural metaphor contributes to the sense of solidity, of enduring existence.

The Durkheimian vision was magnificently elaborated by the *Annales* historians in their exploration of the *longue durée* of historical continuity, and their search for the deeper reality underlying superficial events. It finds perhaps its most famous expression in Le Roy Ladurie's concept of *l'histoire immobile*. Nationalist histories frequently proclaim such long-term continuities, beyond the turbulent changes of politics. Braudel's *L'Identité de la France*, which points to the underlying structures of continuity in the regional identities of the country over many centuries, is a masterpiece of this genre (1986).

Lévi-Straussian structuralism in one way offers another version of 'motionless' temporality, in so far as it privileges the synchronic, and professes indifference to change or even time. The underlying structures of human thought which are his main concern are in his view not subject to the contingencies of time and space. However, at another level Lévi-Strauss aligns himself with the discourse of modernism; he partially undermines the radical nature of his position by emphasising the difference between the primitive and 'us', articulated at different points in his work as the contrasted modes of representing and experiencing historical time (cold versus hot), or the effects of literacy, or a contrast in kinship structures (elementary versus complex). None the less, his position emphasises not so much a temporality of rupture as a paradigmatic discontinuity between the concern with structure and continuity on the part of the 'savage mind', and the privileging of constant change in our own civilisation.

The postmodern moment

The predominant temporality of the present time is one of fluidity and indeterminacy, rather than linear continuity or a systematic contrast between past and present. The postmodern moment emphasises the particularity of events and is profoundly sceptical both of any postulate of continuity and of generalising projects. Where there is evidence of continuities, these are interpreted ironically as the result of a constant process of re-creation, rather than as repetition or the inert presence of the past. The current orthodoxy within anthropology emphasises flux and change as a constant process; agency is emphasised in contrast – indeed in opposition to – structure, and performance, voice and poetics have replaced a concern with text. There is an insistence on movement, on change, on impermanence. This moment is typically evoked through terms such as emergence, creation, contestation, empowerment, negotiation, indeterminacy, reinvention and transformation, and its critiques of earlier anthropological models focus particularly on the problems of essentialism and determinism.

Alongside this general move against reification, not only of tradition but also of culture, society and structure in general, there is also a tendency to privilege the marginal. Boundedness, holism and continuity are seen as ideological creations, the mythologising postulates of dominant groups, while the qualities of discontinuity and fragmentation typical of the postmodern moment are found most explicitly in the margins, the periphery (Rosaldo 1989).

The concern with fluidity and constant change has often been identified as the hallmark of modernity, notably in Marshall Berman's influential study (1983). However the 'postmodern moment' defined as a distinctive sense of temporality in anthropology does not identify fluidity as a symptom of modernity, but rather claims it to be a universal property of human societies and culture. Its view of temporality rejects any dichotomised perspective. Whereas the modernist moment emphasises present change in contrast to a static past, the postmodern moment as I am identifying it denies that the past was ever static, and hypostatises fluidity and change as a permanent condition. It seeks to break the old Eurocentric idea that 'we' have history but 'they' don't, and has developed alongside the return to history on the part of the social sciences. In contrast to the 'allochrony' of modernism, this moment is typified by 'coevalness' in anthropological discourse, advocated by Johannes Fabian as the appropriate antidote to allochrony (1983). That is, an ethical and literary concern to recognise the shared temporality that joins the anthropologist and those she or he studies, and an emphasis on the impact of the global system in bringing all the world's populations into a single time-frame.

There are many intellectual sources which have contributed to this rethinking, ranging from World Systems theory which emphasises the complementarity and simultaneity of different economic forms in contrast to a more linear model of economic change, to the post-structuralist interest in strategies for power, and in demystifying tradition as a means of domination. It is symptomatic of the current intellectual climate that it is hard to use the concepts of tradition or custom without irony, usually signalled by a distancing device: 'tradition', so-called custom, and so on. It is a curious reflection of the contemporary undoing of Enlightenment certainties that it is almost easier at present to speak of magic without self-consciousness or embarrassment than to talk of tradition. None the less the concept of tradition returns again and again in spite of this unease, evoking all the ambivalence of the relationship with the past that must typify the life of any cultural formation.

Proponents of what I am labelling the postmodern moment frequently criticise 'modernist' and 'structuralist' temporalities as unhistorical, in that they invoke some timeless essence instead of recognising the way that all aspects of culture and society are in motion, *even when the actors themselves proclaim continuity.*[7] They draw on historical data in order to reveal discontinuities, the inventedness of peoples' visions of the past. It could be argued that the postmodern moment seeks to replace the concept of tradition with an open-ended 'history' in the sense of ongoing change as the primary object of study. However, postmodern historicity aims at demystifying and deconstructing, revealing the context-boundedness of eternal verities and the shallow time depth of supposedly long-term traditions, in short at historicising rather than constructing a narrative of linear unfolding in the more conventional sense of history.

THE REFUSAL OF OBJECTIFICATION

The postmodern critique offers a necessary corrective to the kinds of immobilism and indifference to historical change that anthropology has so often exhibited. Moreover, anthropological categories have in many instances hovered ambiguously between scientific objectivity and echoing the discourse of those whom we study, particularly the more articulate of our informants. This point has recently been made to good effect by students of nationalism. Handler, for example, has argued that the anthropological conception of culture arose in the nineteenth century out of many of the same sources as nationalist ideas, and often remains complicit with them to the present day (1988). Not only nationalism, but also anthropology, typically objectifies and reifies culture, although the current interest among anthropologists in studying nationalist movements reflects some degree of distancing from this previous complicity. A similar argument can be made with respect to tradition, which is also salient in nationalist discourses.[8] The concept of tradition preceded the development of anthropology and helped to define a field for it as a distinctive form of knowledge. However anthropological research has also renewed it and given it greater substance and apparent objectivity. It is surely this mutual reinforcement that renders tradition such an appealing and yet troubling concept for anthropologists.

It is partly in the recognition of these complicities that the critique of concepts such as tradition has developed, pointing to the objectification of tradition and culture by ethnic nationalisms whose legitimacy rests on a selective mythologisation of the past. Those nationalists who most vehemently proclaim the continuities of their cultural traditions are those whose personal life-trajectories are the most fractured, most remote from the supposedly stable agrarian communities from which the discourse of tradition usually derives. The most extreme forms of traditionalism today are often found amongst 'long-distance nationalists' separated from their homeland, whose invocation of traditions in an alien context is a palpable reinvention (Anderson 1992; also Appadurai 1990).

But it is not just the study of ethnicity and nationalism that gives rise to this type of critique. In a broader context, many anthropologists now argue that all reification of culture is alien to the indeterminacy of social life. So for example, Ronald Inden in *Imagining India* (1990) has advanced an eloquent critique of the ways that India both past and present has over the centuries solidified into a timeless essence in European representations of it (what he terms Indology). Inden argues that such a configuration is not only unhistorical, but also invidious in that it fails to recognise the agency of the subordinate Indian population. It is an 'imperial knowledge' based on the methods of natural science, which displaces the agency of Indians on to timeless essences or directly on to their western rulers. But in making this argument he gives little recognition to the ways that India's ruling groups were as much implicated as European administrators and writers in promoting an essentialised view of Indian history and society (Burghart 1990). European rule was only one in a long line of different forms of domination. The ruling groups in so far as they denied agency to their subordinates were manifesting their own agency (Bayly 1990).

The concept of codification has also been the subject of similar critique. For example, Talal Asad points to the way that in anglophone

Africa it was the colonial administrators with their bureaucratic expectations who used a particular notion of custom or tradition to codify the practices of the colonised. In so doing, the British in Africa reified the fluid, context-bound practices of lineage elders into what became known as customary law, and anthropologists mistakenly believed that what they observed was an unbroken tradition, instead of the particular effects of colonial rule. They were therefore unable to see the 'indeterminate, contradictory and open-ended character of social structures' (Asad 1991: 321–2).

Bourdieu, who is a major theoretical source for the postmodern moment, has denounced codification as part of the discipline of the great state bureaucracies. In his view codification, that is, legalism and rules, is oppressive while the habitus is associated with vagueness and indeterminacy. In his characterisation of codification we can see a fundamental antagonism to the state as a political form, and even to the practice of writing itself (1990).

The refusal of codification has a double meaning in so far as it refers to the anthropological enterprise. On the one hand anthropology is itself a codifying practice and a symptom of what Bourdieu is seeking to distance himself from. On the other, historically it has given special attention to subordinated groups, and is predisposed to locate and to criticise the effects of power. Asad associates codification particularly with the alien impositions of colonial government, but Bourdieu's position identifies codification with the exercise of power more broadly, for which he reveals a fundamental mistrust.

For 'modernists' and 'structuralists' the stable community bound by tradition matched their intellectual needs. By contrast, the 'post-modernists' tend to valorise social situations of fragmentation, marginality and hybridity. But this particular emphasis arises not only from an ethical position of giving recognition to the subordinate, but also from an empirical and a philosophical argument, to the effect that contrary to the postulates of classical anthropology, social behaviour is not rule-governed.

These positions which privilege fluidity and transformation accord well with the current tempo of globalisation. However, they leave open the question of continuities. The proclivity of anthropological discourse to perceive essences was not merely the illusion of a scientific discipline. It was also the product in many instances of the way anthropologists chose their principal informants, who might for a variety of reasons legitimate their practices or identify themselves in terms of a particular relationship with the past. It was not simply an invention by anthropologists and folklorists that the people whom they were studying often explained and justified their present practices with reference to the wisdom of the ancestors, or to the need to observe certain taboos, or simply to custom. The temporality of the postmodern moment, then, is not only challenging the temporalities of much previous anthropological writing, but is also recontextualising the testimonies of our informants.

Concepts such as essentialism, objectification or codification are all identifiable by means of a contrast with flux and indeterminacy. However they are not synonymous and tradition can be related to them in differing ways. Essentialism, with its denial of historical change and human agency, is certainly typical of 'imperial knowledge' as Inden claims, but it is also a much more general characteristic of social discourse. Whenever people claim that they do things the way the ancestors taught them, they are using essentialist language, denying their own agency. All assertions of continuity with the past (such as those which are typical of religious discourse) are essentialist in this sense. By contrast, objectification and codification are more limited in their implications. Codification, as the formalisation of rules of social behaviour, develops in particular historical circumstances. It often invokes a sense of continuity with the past (e.g. in religious laws) but does not necessarily do so. For example, the codifications of Roman law are based on a set of clearly enunciated principles, in contrast to those of common law which derive from precedents from the past. Objectification is the process whereby cultures or traditions are conceptualised as thing-like, identifiable and observable as stable, bounded wholes. This involves a level of self-consciousness which again arises in particular historical contexts often, but not exclusively, associated with ethnic or nationalist movements.

RETHINKING CONTINUITY AND CHANGE

To argue as postmodernists do for a temporality of fluctuation is a form of reductionism, since it fails to recognise the ways that different social groups – and not only in conditions of modernity – defend continuity, and their rights to claim and express particular links with the past. It can be agreed that any claim concerning an objectified tradition, any invocation of continuity with a distant past is likely to have a political intent. As a consequence, it is subject to contestation by those whose interests it infringes. However it must be borne in mind that it is not only strategies for domination which essentialise the past, but also strategies for the defence of customary rights. Codification may reduce people's room for manoeuvre ('strategising' in Bourdieu's terminology), but it also offers some protection to the subordinate. An obvious example is that of land rights. In countless situations across the world, peoples' and groups' maintenance of rights to land depends on their being able to demonstrate continuity with the past. This is particularly important in situations where no written documents exist to 'prove' such continuity. This is not new: in medieval English law the defence of customary rights was based on the same principle, invoked by the telling phrase 'since the time whereof the memory of man runneth not to the contrary'.[9]

In contrast to the refusal of tradition and continuity typical in different ways of both modern and postmodern temporalities, a positive reading of the concept has been offered by some contemporary philosophers, notably Hans-Georg Gadamer (1975) and Alistair Macintyre (1985), which can be characterised by the idea of 'living tradition'. It stands in marked contrast to the static vision of tradition that we have inherited from the nineteenth century, and instead emphasises the inherent debatability of the past (see also Appadurai 1981). The past is not entirely 'other' for the present, nor is it merely a source of mystification, but is also the ground for the present. According to this position, the current emphasis on change and on reason is partly illusory: we are more connected to the past than we recognise.

The converse of tradition is change. To discuss the concept of tradition is to interrogate the very category of change, and beyond that the possible forms in which a relationship with the past can be conceived and lived. The postulate of change is necessary in order to uncover the 'inventedness' of tradition, and to reveal how rarely claims of unbroken continuity from the past can be sustained. Perhaps in a similar way tradition can be a means of interrogating the concept of change, which is so fundamental to the cosmology of modernity. One of the consequences of the postmodern moment in anthropology, it seems to me, is that we have become very much more aware of how *ad hoc* and untheorised are our ideas about change. What was described a generation ago as stability and continuity is now described as change. Moreover, change is usually assumed to be self-evident. In either case, the criteria employed by anthropologists themselves usually take precedence over the categories of those whose life they were describing. Part of the issue is that social scientists' indicators of change or stability may be very different from those of other social agents, privileging macro-social, political and economic structures the way they define continuity, and alterations in such structures indicators of change. For ordinary people on the other hand, it is as likely to be a particular ritual performance, or the texture of everyday life that signifies stability and continuity and its opposite.[10] People may invoke tradition in doing something that to the outside observer seems innovative, and conversely they may claim novelty for something that to the outside observer does not seem new. It is a not uncommon experience for anthropologists today to think they are witnessing irreversible change in what they are studying, and yet to be told by the local people themselves that nothing has changed, that in key respects everything has remained the same.[11]

Rather than dismissing such responses as a nostalgic clinging on to a vanishing past, examples like these might lead us to a more nuanced reading of tradition. In order to unpack the very different meanings that may be invoked by the term, we need to distinguish several modalities of discourse concerning the past. First, there is objectivist anthropology and history, which seek to establish whether or not claims for continuities with the past can be substantiated by the historical record. Second, there are the objectification and codification of the past that occur in some historical conditions, but do not include all claims about continuity with the past. Third, there is the concept of 'living tradition' which refuses the absolute dichotomised understanding of the opposition between continuity and change and asserts that change is grounded in continuities. Fourth, there are claims about continuity with the past which certain groups and individuals assert within a particular social context, invoking a particular language of legitimation.

The attempt to use concepts of tradition and change in an absolutist way, as though they could possibly have a universal and objective status, is flawed in itself. We should instead recognise that they are bound to particular contexts. The variability in notions of change and continuity, flux and stability, should be taken seriously not only for general methodological reasons, but also because they embody constitutive features of local practice. In arguing this I do not wish to imply that local contexts are divorced from wider social and semantic structures, but to underline the point that discourses of continuity and change are not as universal and objective as they may appear. Some aspects of social life may alter without causing more than ripples around them, whereas others are implicated in the central categories that define a particular social environment. If we seek to investigate which are the elements that are constitutive in this way, we will perhaps come closer to understanding the ambiguities, and temporalities, of tradition and change, and in so doing redefine and clarify their use as anthropological concepts.[12]

NOTES

1 I do not here consider the differences between anthropology and ethnology, for example, or the closely related field of folklore studies, since my aim in this chapter is not to give a historical account but to draw attention to some very general implications of the ways that traditions have been studied.

2 Giddens avoids the term tradition itself, but his ill-defined concept of the 'pre-modern' fulfils the same discursive functions, especially since it is identified solely in terms of its temporal relationship to modernity. However other Weberians, notably E. Shils, have not discussed the concept in depth (1981). It should be added of course that while Weber himself devoted little attention to tradition as a distinctive concept, it was crucial in his typology of forms of dominance and legitimation, particularly as a contrast to charismatic and bureaucratic domination to which he did devote more sustained attention. Moreover, his studies of Islam and China are empirical analyses of tradition as a form of domination.

3 In an early passage Malinowski writes: 'every item of culture . . . represents a value, fulfils a social function . . . For tradition is a fabric in which all the strands are so clearly woven that the destruction of one unmakes the whole' (cited in Asad 1991).

4 This association is central to European sociological and anthropological thought (Tönnies, Durkheim, Weber, Marx and Dumont). Marilyn Strathern has recently pointed out, however, that a tradition can also be individualist, for example, the English (1992).

5 Why this should be particularly associated with the French intellectual culture – since after all it was the French who invented revolutions – is an interesting question in the history of ideas.

6 See the preface to the first number of *Annales* (1896); also Burke (1990: 9) and Giddens (1977: 234–71) for Durkheim's dismissal of the French Revolution as symptom rather than cause of social change.

7 Pascal Boyer has advanced an interesting theory of tradition which starts from the opposite position. Rather than denying continuity, he takes it as an obvious fact, and investigates the cognitive mechanisms by which repetition takes place, particularly in the context of religious discourse. He too discounts people's own explanations as to why they repeat traditions, but on the grounds that they are implausible in terms of cognitive psychology (1990).

8 For some anthropologists, the concept of tradition is restricted to this objectified sense in the context of developing ethnic or nationalist consciousness (e.g. Linnekin 1983; Linnekin and Poyer 1990).

9 I am grateful to Heinz Lubasz for this example. It should of course be recognised at the same time that the discourse of rights for some that is constituted by codification and custom at the same time exludes others.

10 Collard illustrates this in her account of indigenous understandings of twentieth-century historical process in a Greek village (1989).
11 There is a telling example in a recent documentary film about the Kayapo Indians of Brazilian Amazonia. In the terms of the film-maker, the anthropologist (Terry Turner) and the presumed audience, the subject of the film was the dramatic changes that had occurred in Kayapo life over the past 20 years. But counterintuitively the Kayapo, investing their new-found wealth in ever more elaborate performances of rituals, insisted that on the contrary that nothing had changed.
12 This is a substantially revised version of the paper presented in the symposium organised by Peter Skalník at the EASA Conference in Prague. I am grateful to the Anthropology Department of the University of Oslo for giving me the opportunity to teach a course on the politics of tradition, and to students and colleagues for many insights and discussions. I also wish to thank the Anthropology seminar of the University of Tromsø for their critical comments, and especially Per Mathiesen for a detailed and helpful discussion of the issues.

REFERENCES

Anderson, B. (1992) 'The new world disorder', New Left Review, 193 (May–June): 3–14.
Appadurai, A. (1981) 'The past as a scarce resource', Man 16(2): 201–19.
—— (1990) 'Disjuncture and difference in the global cultural economy', in M. Featherstone, Global Culture, London: Sage.
Ardener, E. (1989) 'Social anthropology and the decline of modernism', in The Voice of Prophecy, Oxford: Blackwell, pp. 191–210.
Asad, T. (1991) 'Afterword: from the history of colonial anthropology to the anthropology of western hegemony', in G. Stocking (ed.), Colonial Situations, History of Anthropology vol. 7, Wisconsin: University of Wisconsin Press, pp. 314–24.
Bayly, C. A. (1990) Review of Imagining India, by R. Inden, Times Literary Supplement, 1313 (7–13 Dec.).
Berman, M. (1983) All that is Solid Melts into Air, London: Verso.
Bourdieu, P. (1990) 'Codification', in In Other Words: Essays Towards a Reflexive Sociology, Oxford: Polity, pp. 76–86.
Boyer, P. (1990) Tradition as Truth and as Communication, Cambridge: Cambridge University Press.
Braudel, F. (1986) L'Identité de la France, Paris: Arthaud-Flammarion.
Burghart, R. (1990) 'Ethnographers and their local counterparts in India', in R. Fardon (ed.), Localizing Stratiegies: Regional Traditions of Ethnographic Writing, Edinburgh: Scottish Academic Press.
Burke, P. (1990) The French Historical Revolution, Oxford: Polity.
Collard, A. (1989) 'Investigating "social memory" in a Greek context', in E. Tonkin, M. Macdonald and M. Chapman (eds), History and Ethnicity, ASA Monographs No. 27, London: Routledge, pp. 89–103.
Fabian, J. (1983) Time and the Other, New York: Columbia University Press.
Gadamer, H.-G. (1975) Truth and Method, New York: Seabury Press.

Giddens, A. (1977) 'Durkheim's political sociology', in *Studies in Social and Political Theory*, London: Hutchinson, pp. 234–71.
—— (1990) *The Consequences of Modernity*, Oxford: Polity.
Handler, R. (1988) *Nationalism and the Politics of Culture in Quebec*, Madison: University of Wisconsin Press.
Inden, R. (1990) *Imagining India*, Oxford: Oxford University Press.
Kern, S. (1983) *The Culture of Time and Space*, London: Weidenfeld.
Kuper, A. (1988) *The Invention of Primitive Society*, London: Routledge.
Linnekin, J. (1983) 'Defining tradition: variations on the Hawaiian identity', *American Ethnologist* 10(2): 241–52.
Linnekin, J. and Poyer, L. (eds) (1990) *Cultural Identity and Ethnicity in the Pacific*, Honolulu: University of Hawaii Press.
Macintyre, A. (1985) *After Virtue: A Study in Moral Theory*, London: Duckworth.
Osborne, P. (1992) 'Modernity is a qualitative, not a chronological category', *New Left Review*, 192 (March–April): 65–84.
Robertson, R. (1990) 'After nostalgia? Wilful nostalgia and the phases of globalisation', in B. Turner (ed.), *Theories of Modernity and Postmodernity*, London: Sage.
Rosaldo, R. (1989) *Culture and Truth*, Boston: Beacon Press.
Sahlins, M. (1991) 'The return of the event, again', in A. Biersack (ed.), *Clio in Oceania*, Washington: Smithsonian Institution.
Shils, E. (1981) *Tradition*, London: Faber.
Strathern, M. (1992) *After Nature*, Cambridge: Cambridge University Press.

Chapter 2

The present
A bridge between the past and the future

Václav Hubinger

In principle, it does not seem possible to strictly separate – both in 'reality' and analysis – the past, the present and the future. These three temporalities are neither clearly delimited nor clearly delimitable since more than anything else they represent culturally unique, political and social contexts that follow one another in time. The picture of each one of these contexts is conceptualised either in the following (i.e. 'the past' is created in 'the present'), or in the preceding ('the future' is created in 'the present'), and is subject to continuous reassessment which is, naturally enough, also situated in 'the present'. The inherent paradoxes of this 'present' include the fact that each 'present' was once the future and will become the past.

In this chapter I would like to show the role that ethnography[1] played in the process of creating a picture of the modern Czech nation's past, and how it participated in the realisation of its 'future'. I will not specifically consider the role and position of this discipline in the Czech Republic today, where the national function of ethnography is after all somewhat weaker than in Slovakia. The search for national identity and its expression in Slovakia has recently culminated in the foundation of a nation-state. Although the same thing happened to the Czechs, this was something of a defeat rather than the achievement they had wished for. Nevertheless, in spite of the frequent proclamations emphasising the priority of the civic principle (understood in opposition to the national principle) today's Czech society in its nation-state (the first since the beginning of the seventeenth century) drinks – at least in reminiscences – from the spring provided by ethnographers and folklorists.

I

Ethnography in its Czech conception is closely related to folklore studies and together they form a discipline called *národopis* (a Czech calque of the Greek term *ethnographia* and identical in content with the German *Volkskunde*). In the nineteenth century, ethnography was one of the most important instruments of the evolving nationalism. It assisted this process contributing the main representations. These served to both assert and constantly affirm the reality of an up until then, non-existent product.

Protagonists in the nineteenth-century movement characterised the present (viewed as a situational context) by highlighting the then obvious non-existence of a Czech political nation, which was still only the future (see Hobsbawm 1991: 9). The Czech nationalist movement and Czech nationalism came into being within the context of contemporary European thinking, especially German. The very term ethnography meaning *Volkskunde* was taken from the German intellectual milieu (Vermeulen 1992). The cultural and intellectual atmosphere of the then Central Europe was dominated by Romanticism, particularly in the German-speaking and German-dominated areas (the educated people in the Czech Lands either spoke only German or were bilingual). The works of Johann Joachim Winckelmann (1717–68) and subsequently Johann Wolfgang Goethe (1749–1832), and especially those of Johann Gottfried Herder (1744–1803), were of great influence. Herder's conviction that it is language and tradition that create a nation (Herder 1941) proved to be not only exceptionally influential, but dangerous, given the consequences of his thesis, that is, a nation's right to self-determination (see Hubinger 1992). His assessment of the Slavs as the 'Greeks of the modern age' must have been music to the ears of the nationalist 'awakeners'. Did not this metaphor embrace both the 'great past of Europe', the very foundations of its – and so effectively the world's – civilisation and the vision of the grand future of the oppressed nations'?

It should not be forgotten that national history and geography[2] also contributed to the construction of Czech national identity, and especially to the image of an idealised Czech identity. Czech *Volkskunde* (at first dominated by folklore studies, later on by ethnography) was born as an inseparable and fundamental part of a process called 'national revival' (see Československá vlastivěda 1968; Horák 1933; Robek 1979). It would be more accurate to speak of the 'nascence', rather than 'revival', of the Czech nation since – as we have said – there was not a true Czech nation prior to that. Yet, in a way, the use of the word is symptomatic, as 'revival' quite unambiguously conjures up the idea of something that had been here before but does not exist 'now'. The past existence of a given entity confers the right, as it were, to bring it into life, or rather revive it, while the making of something new, unprecedented, may of course raise doubts. Thus the process of revival is in fact the renewal of order, the emergence of anything new is usually connected with change, with the demise of something else, and hence with chaos and the disruption of the existing order of things.

The concept of 'revival' was to express that the Czech nation (in the sense of the Czech-speaking and Czech-thinking population of the then Czech kingdom) existed before 1620, a year which symbolises the beginning of 'three centuries of subjugation' (until 1918), and that it is now undergoing revival, emerging from 'oblivion' and freeing itself from oppression. The nationalist movement of the nineteenth century set itself the goal of reviving the nation as a political reality and experts (at least in our country) are still arguing over the actual periodisation of this process, that is, when it began and what might be regarded as its end (see Hroch 1986). These discussions are part of the process of making 'history', and naturally ethnography also has a say in this because Czech folk culture is regarded as its chief object of study. The fact that these discussions take place even today, cannot be considered paradoxical since the renewed Czech state (quite a common phrase on our contemporary political scene) must continue to look after its 'national cultural heritage'. Ethnography, which, to a large extent, has been a co-maker of this heritage, is today responsible for its protection and scientific analysis. In a way, the ethnographers of the nineteenth and the early twentieth centuries, who were creating the nation's past, saw to the jobs of their professional followers in the future.

One of the main goals of Czech *Volkskunde* in the early stages of the national movement was to save the Czech language which in turn was to become the basis for the creation of a nation. In accordance with Herder's ideas the national language – its standardised, written form, as distinct from its colloquial forms – was constructed by intellectuals. They used these very colloquial language forms and a 200-year-old translation of the Bible (not a particularly exceptional procedure, as is generally known; see Anderson 1991: 72–5; Falla 1991: 220–40).

In the nineteenth-century Czech Lands the Czech-speaking, and therefore 'Czech' population (according to Herderian criteria) consisted only, and as the better part, of the rural inhabitants of central areas (the frontier regions and many towns were largely German). In the nationalist discussions these Czech-speaking peasants were inevitably conceptualised as a 'folk' (see on this Hubinger 1990; Lass 1989) – and, in keeping with Herder and the Romantics, as the core of the nation, its sound and uncorrupted basis. Some features of this folk culture and way of life were even regarded as the continuation of ancient Czech culture from the mythical pre-Christian era. As a matter of fact, this era was also constructed by the nationalist Romantics as the incipient period of Czech history. The whole process of making a 'folk' and nation's past began at a time when such sciences as archaeology and art history came into being, inspired by Macpherson's 'discovery' of the Poems of Ossian.[3]

Another logical step that the revivalists took was the discovery and expression of 'tradition'. To preserve the folk language and culture as the basis of a Czech national culture also meant to collect (in the positivist spirit, thus verify) and present in public as much 'traditional' material as possible. Only through public presentation supplemented by an appropriate explanation could these constructions become a reality, and even part of the consumers' 'present'. These efforts culminated in the Czechoslavic Ethnographic Exhibition of 1895. This gigantic under-taking (see Národopisná výstava Českoslovanská v Praze 1895, 1895a, 1895b) had been preceded by several years of intensive collection of materials and their presentation at regional exhibitions. (In many cases these collections form the basis of the ethnographic collections of regional museums in Bohemia, Moravia and Silesia.)[4] The objects and additional documentation collected were interpreted not only as the signs of genuine folk culture, but also as throwbacks to the past. (Unfortunately, this was probably the only case where Czech *Volkskunde* took inspiration from social anthropology.) As relics of the genuine and authentic spirit of an era they were sometimes regarded as regrettably spoiled by the destructive effects of German, or urban culture. It was this collecting activity, its regional, social and ethnic orientations (all of which naturally had a deep influence on what was being collected), and the great political and commercial success of the the the 1895 exhibition, that set the image of Czech folk culture for the next hundred years.[5]

The Czechoslavic Ethnographic Exhibition of 1895, a truly historic event from the point of view of the further political development of Czech society and ethnography, was held in a place that had several times played a comparatively significant role in the formation of Czech national as well as international consciousness. In 1891 this place was the site of a large industrial show which presented Czech society as manifestly self-confident and economically developed. (It is hard to resist reference to the work of Hobsbawm and Ranger 1983.) The exhibition of 1895 was in fact the realisation of the notions concerning Czech folk culture as the basis of an *already* existing political nation. Between the two world wars the Exhibition Ground was the site of industrial shows and trade fairs; during the Nazi occupation it housed the propaganda exposition 'The Soviet Paradise' (1942). The connection of the Exhibition Ground with the ideological education of the population became even stronger after the Communist take-over in 1948. It was a meeting place for the Communist Party, trade union congresses, and so-called popular festivals on various holidays (such as May Day celebrations and the Day of the Press, an anniversary of the Communist Party daily *Rudé právo*). The purpose of these events was always to signify the close connection of the ruling circles with 'folk' (although the idea of 'folk' or 'people' was different from that of the Romanticism of the nineteenth century). This tendency was unintentionally strengthened in the 1960s when the fair of St Matthew (after St Matthew's Church in another part of Prague), probably the most 'folkish' annual entertainment in Prague, was moved to this site. Since the 1989 revolution things have gone on unchanged – in addition to St Matthew's fairs, the General Industrial Show was held here in 1991 to commemorate the hundred years since the 1891 Show, and to throw 'into relief' the new, and once again, self-confident Czechoslovakia. Both this show and the Car Show held shortly afterwards were generally chaotic, disgracing the organisers (Prague municipality, some other state institutions and private companies).

The 1895 Ethnographic Exhibition reinforced and confirmed what ethnographers and historians had long before been communicating to the general public through all possible media. The folk with its reputedly sterling proto-Slavic and old Czech cultural features was recognised as the core of the Czech nation. A number of the cultural characteristics that were reputedly or actually found in a relatively small group of peasants (well-to-do, or at least comfortably situated, farmers characterised by self-confidence, ostentatious consumption and emphasis on external appearances manifest in representative festive costumes and behaviour[6]) were taken over, in the process of nation-building by other social groups – especially in towns and cities – as contextual and occasional signs of their Czech identity (and affiliation) and folk character. Both qualities were regarded as positive values without which national identity was unthinkable.

This resulted in the concept of folk (accepted by the nationally conscious part of Czech society) as the core of the nation, as the bearer of the truest and best traditions. Folk personified the past of the nation (not its 'historical' but 'cultural' past), and its ethnic and cultural continuity going back to the remotest imaginable past.

II

The results of ethnographic and folklorc studies were published not only in specialist literature (in 1891 a journal, still in existence, was founded, with the symptomatic title *Český lid*, 'The Czech Folk'), but also in popular magazines and newspapers. The work of the scholars then encountered such enthusiastic response from the public then that their counterparts today may rightly feel envious. All this contributed to the creation of 'imagined community' which was conscious of its Czech identity transformed into Czech national consciousness defined ethnically (i.e. primarily in terms of language), culturally (by means of Czech folk culture) and with a strong political charge. The basis of national consciousness was non-national, not explicitly expressed (unless confronted by another identity), Czech identity was one of the many identities of the population in the Czech Lands. National Czech identity, that is politically charged Czech identity, derived part of its justification from facts such as the indisputably long existence of the state (i.e. the Kingdom of Bohemia) in the Middle Ages.[7] The nation as a cultural and political community began to represent 'the present', and an independent nation-state was its 'future' (in the case of the Czechs, so distant that the first serious attempts at achieving political independence emerge as late as the first years of World War I).

The reality of German nationalism and the political and economic position of the Czechs in Austria, or Austria-Hungary, in the nineteenth century with their own nationalism gave rise to the once widespread, and still recognised, belief that the history of the Czechs is in fact the history of the struggle between Slavic and German elements, a struggle that has been going on for centuries.[8] The interpretation of nineteenth- and twentieth-century Czech reality ('the present' of the nationalists and revivalists) was also affected by these beliefs, which contributed both to the making and to the stabilisation of this reality. The creation of independent Czechoslovakia in 1918 was the climax of the Czech nationalists' efforts and, in a sense, should have signified the end of their 'present' – for at that moment they entered 'the future'.

By contrast with our everyday experience, it seems that in the nationalists' argument, 'the present' is not fully conceptualised and represented. Nationalists (nationally conscious enthusiasts as well as those who are only passive consumers of their ideology) fight for the fulfilment of their wishes, for the achievement of the longed-for goal. For them the past seems to be separated from the present, and the future is barely visible somewhere in the far distance.

The nationalists had the good fortune to live to see the fulfilment, the arrival of the future; on the declaration of independence of 'their' nation-state. Until that moment the independent nation-state was the future, the present was its non-existence and the efforts to create it; and the past was all that was used as arguments to justify its independence. The achievement of independence makes the former 'present' of the nationalists part of their own heroic past, and the former future becomes the present ('reality'). Since they move along in the evolutionist pattern, they still have enough leeway for the next future, to improve upon the 'present' condition. This may be seen as the point of contact between nationalist and Communist thinking: linear development runs from the mythical harmonious past through periods of disharmony and unfreedom, through phases of a struggle for liberty down to the final deliverance and the enhancement of success. This, essentially dramatic, construction of the process of development is strongly reminiscent of mythological, fairytale and Messianic formulas, and even the use of military terminology – fight, advancement, enemies, and so on – is far from accidental (see Macura 1992: 19–22).

The problem which any nationalism (and anyone dealing with nationalism) has to face is the obvious fact that nationalism (unlike the student of nationalism) should, as a matter of fact, lose its *raison d'être* once it reaches its proclaimed goal. But, as is well known, the birth of a nation and of a nation-state is by no means the end of nationalism and its advocates. On the contrary: the very fact of the creation of a nation and a nation-state represents only a transitional phase in the process which started in the past and which – as any past – extends, through its intentions, through the present into the future. The future was formulated in the past and is subject to reformulation in the present, according to the changing circumstances, depending on how the past is being construed and interpreted.

III

In 1918, the reality of the fledgling Czechoslovakia bore the seeds of all its subsequent problems. The unification of the Czech Lands (Bohemia, Moravia and part of Silesia) with Slovakia and Sub-Carpathian

Ruthenia (these last two were part of the Hungarian state for a thousand years) was a pragmatic political step, reflecting a 100-year-old nationalist attitude. The Slovaks, having survived the thousand years of Hungarian domination and strong Hungarisation, had, since the nineteenth century, been regarded as natural allies of the Czechs. The Czechs, on the other hand, had gone through a thousand-year struggle against the 'German element' and three centuries of re-catholicisation and Germanisation. The union of the Czechs and the Slovaks was to have resulted in a united Czechoslovak nation, composed of two branches, each one retaining its own language and cultural identity. The idea of a Czechoslovak nation was a construction that was intended to create a sufficiently strong national community that would outnumber the Germans (who were·more numerous in Czechoslovakia at that time than the Slovaks) and the Hungarians. The aim was to create such conditions in which neither Germans nor Hungarians – eventually, nor the Slovaks – could demand autonomy.

The size and economic and political strength of the German community, partly composed of Jews, kept alive the old antagonism which propaganda presented as being age-old and natural. The bitter, and as it were, confirming proof of it was the destruction of Czechoslovakia in 1938 (interpreted by Sudeten Germans as the result of the anti-German policy of the Czechoslovak government), followed by the Nazi occupation between 1939 and 1945. The post-war expulsion of Germans from Czechoslovakia must therefore be seen not only as retaliation for those who suffered in the war, or, as a condemnable effort to seize something at the expense of people affected by war (which certainly was the case of Sudeten Germans and Czechoslovak Germans in general). It was, at the same time, an abhorrent outcome of a century-old and on-going process of intensive self-conviction that the Czechs and the Germans represent two essentially distinct ethnic communities which cannot peacefully co-exist within the same state.

The conscience of ethnography in this respect is not exactly snow white. It had successfully convinced people that there was a genuine and 'purely' Czech culture, diametrically opposed to the culture of 'the others', represented primarily by the geographically closest, and yet vastly dissimilar neighbours – the Germans and the Jews. (The same applies to the ethnography of those 'others', see Gajek 1990.) On the other hand, the similarities, both real and apparent (in the eyes of nationalism just as real), with Slavic cultures, especially Slovak, Polish and Russian, were rated as positive phenomena.

The social and political reality of post-war Czechoslovakia strengthened this Slavic element in the Czech world outlook. Since the Napoleonic Wars Russophilia had been an important part of it, and in World War II, too, Germany was defeated by the 'Russians' (as was the general term for the Soviet Army) who liberated Czechoslovakia. The early 1950s, in many ways a terrible period for not only Central Europe, introduced a number of new ideas, though often under old labels, into ethnography. The national element began to be suppressed (at least in the rhetoric of the up-coming generation of scholars), and crucial emphasis was placed on a class-based approach in the spirit of Marxist-Leninist precepts about proletarian internationalism and the progressive role of the masses in world history. It required only a small step to move from conceiving of folk as representing the past condition of a nation to viewing it as representative of the working masses – the ruling power in the 'present' of the 1950s in communist countries. Nationalism also represented folk as the producer of material values (even today one of the most popular metaphors in our country is that of the 'golden Czech hands' and the inseparable quality of the true Czech spirit is the industriousness of 'our people'), and so in this respect it was not in conflict with the class-based approach of Marxists-Leninists. It appeared that for certain groups within (ethnographic) folk and for certain values of its culture it was enough to add an appropriate evaluation, or at least *epitheton ornans*, and the conception of the past could remain basically unchanged, at least as far as ethnography was concerned – otherwise the 'old orders' deserved nothing but condemnation for being 'anti-popular'.

The subject of ethnographic study was still folk or people with the attribute 'working' instead of 'Czech', or rather its previous narrow orientation towards Czech identity was supplemented by the characteristic 'working'. This excluded owners of any means of production from the 'folk', and assigned them to the category of 'exploiters'. They ceased to be 'adored folk' but their cultural characteristics, discovered by nationalists and revivalists, remained subsumed in the notion of 'folkishness'. The presumed characteristics of folk, representing originally the desirable qualities of the whole nation (industriousness, love of peace, indomitability, love of music and singing; how close this was to sociologically seen reality is shown by the observation of the first Czechoslovak president, T. G. Masaryk, that the basis of the future prosperity and self-confidence of the nation should be 'Don't fear and don't steal'), were described as the 'progressive traditions of the working people'. The class-based conception of folk was thus much broader than the previous nationalist one but the purpose for which it was designed was also different. The means, however, remained essentially the same since the aim remained the same: to create an idealised picture of the past (now embodied by 'exploited workers') as the basis of the 'presently' existing reality (proletarians as the ruling class) and the bright future.

In the case of the nation, ideology precedes the reality it speaks of (Gellner 1983) and the same is true of the revolutionary ideology of Marxism-Leninism. In both cases the 'here and now' of its advocates is perceived as a transitional period or phase between the past and the future. The past is a factor determining the shape of their 'present' reality, and the movement of people in the 'present' reality is a factor determining the shape of the 'future'. This future, however, will follow more from the past of the present than from the present. Only when the present becomes the past, will it have a different relationship to the future which in the meantime will become the present. The past present must first become 'history' before it can determine its own future. To create the picture of history based on any ideology requires the existence of a science that will lend credibility to this history (at least that is the case with history within the context of modern western civilisation). Ethnography suited the role perfectly – during the national revival, in pre-war Czechoslovakia, under the Nazis, under the Communists, at any time. The more totalitarian the regime, the less individual freedom and tolerance, the greater the emphasis on the importance of a collective body (national or class), the more successful ethnography and its sister science, folklore studies, were as regards their social appreciation.

Both conceptions of folk – nationalist and class-based – served the political purposes of their time and the communities of the day as they strove to explain the present as a process of fulfilling a purpose, as a developmental phase. Accordingly, development was perceived, and apparently still is, as the difference between the presumed original state (represented by folk culture, national oppression, and exploitation), the 'real' experience of the people of the given period and their vision of the future (i.e. one they were indoctrinated with). At any rate, the element which provided 'flesh and blood' for the ideas of the present was the culturally and contextually determined picture of the past. So far this picture, as produced by ethnography, has passed through three main phases. First, it was folk and its culture seen as the past of a brilliant nation. The next phase was the 'best traditions of the working people'. At present, in connection with the appearance of the modern

Czech state, it is the emphasis on national cultural heritage (whatever that may be) which must be preserved for future generations (again the orientation towards the future). The essential component today is also the representation of Czech cultural identity (this time consciously and intentionally non-national because that might be interpreted as 'backwardness'), conceived as an integral part of the European cultural mosaic.

The ideas representing these three phases are each actively promoted today. The least influential promoters are those who are again invoking Marxist-Leninist slogans, even though phrased in a somewhat reformed spirit. The advocates of the two dominant directions stand in mutual opposition, and naturally enough both are in opposition to Marxists-Leninists.

The 'traditionalist' wing is represented by the majority of Czech ethnographers. They are, as they like to call themselves, 'classical ethnographers'. We will find them not only in museums, faculties and other academic institutions, but also in positions of influence within some civic movements, for example among so-called Moravianists. This, basically political, movement uses a wide range of ethnographic materials (especially those of the 1895 Exhibition) to support their claims of 'Moravian cultural specificity'. No doubt they would protest (at least some of them) against being described here as 'Czech ethnographers' for surely they are Moravians. According to some of them ethnographic data bear out the ethnic uniqueness of Moravians (see on this, Frolec 1991). It is not a necessarily nationalist movement, being more inclined to regionalism and autonomism, but it does show a strong tendency to use nationalist arguments backed up with ethnographic evidence in support of their policy.

The opposite, rather 'modernist', tendency might be called Europeanism. It rejects – openly and volubly – national orientation ('national' in the Central European sense of the word) and attempts to formulate European identity as a positive and desirable value. The assumption is that some time in future (when else) this European identity will overlay all other identities to which it is superordinate. (It has all the makings of a political attitude with an implicit Christian and 'western' orientation.) Not to be accused of 'denationalisation', its advocates speak of the possibility of evolving ethnocultural, non-national (i.e. non-nationalist), yet conscious, Czechness capable of co-existence with other '-nesses' within the same European political and cultural sphere, more or less identical with the EC countries.

IV

Our present is steeped in the past to such an extent that it has become an axiomatically accepted view that we must know our past in order to be able to understand, or interpret our own present. That may even be true, but only inasmuch as we should 'know' the past (i.e. have access to data selected and arranged in a certain way) for the present to make sense, to be understandable and justifiable. The opposite of this would be uprootedness and loss of identity.

The picture of the past is created through data and interpretations which must be supported by 'facts' ('hard data'). For this purpose every culture has developed its own means but no other culture has such a rich arsenal of these means as western, European or Euro-American cultures. We (i.e. both 'we' the anthropologists and contemporary humans) have at our disposal in hypertrophied form what might be called retention media. They include all media that make it possible to record and preserve both expressed and unexpressed ideas that accompany the formation of 'imagined communities'. They include media that can serve as 'materialised memory', from which stored information (or parts of it, purposely selected) may be released 'later on', 'subsequently', in a different context, that means in the future as compared with the time of retention or the past.[9]

The category of retention media in our cultural context comprises books and printed material in general; sound and video records; computerised information; records in long-hand; and so on. They give the process of imagination (i.e. that of creating the imagined community both at individual and collective levels) a time dimension expressed as a distance in time, together with a feeling of change and development. They cause people to 'remember',[10] and hence create imagined communities of (eye)witnesses, contemporaries, or survivors. And so people at the same time 'remember' and reconstruct reality that 'exists no more'. The very act of recollection is something that generates relationships and socially meaningful actions as a result of what has been preserved in memory and, later on, 'retrieved' from it and offered to the public. It goes without saying that every act of remembrance is accompanied by implications based on what is being remembered and in which social and political context.

As an example we may take the recent events, consequences of which have changed the appearance of Czech society and brought about a new wave of processes for which the same name, 'the reassessment of the past', is being used as it was under the Communists (i.e. in 'the past'). It was not by accident that the 1989 non-violent change of regime in Czechoslovakia began on 17 November. Since 1941 this day has been the International Day of Students. It marks the 1939 closure of Czech universities, in the then Protectorate Böhmen und Mähren, followed by executions and imprisonment of the student leaders. The event and the date had lost much of their emotional impact during the communist rule but when the 1989 celebration was disrupted by police violence against the anti-totalitarian protesters, it proved to be a fatal day for the regime. The first reaction of the public was to cry out 'they beat our children' thus drawing a parallel with the way the Nazis once behaved. 'The past', as carefully constructed by Communist propaganda, was based on several focal points, and the anti-Nazi resistance was one of them. After more than forty years of continuous and massive indoctrination people were convinced that they knew quite accurately what happened during the war and, consequently, were able to compare quickly the immediate events with what they knew of the past.

The outcome – not just on the political scene, but in the whole of society – has been an extensive shift in the evaluation of 'historical events', accompanied by the apparent 'remembering' of events and persons that were 'forgotten' and the simultaneous forgetting of those who regarded themselves as unforgettable. Monuments of Communist leaders are now torn down, while monuments of pre-war politicians are re-erected. Elsewhere streets and towns are being renamed, and the property stolen by the previous regime is restored to its original owners. Even religious orders are being given back some of their property. These acts, accompanied by the evocation of a Christian and western (i.e. Catholic and Protestant) orientation of Czech society is indicative of a tendency against an Eastern, Byzantine, and therefore somewhat 'oriental', Christianity. Didn't Communism itself come to us from the 'East'? And so, in a way, all those intellectuals (especially fine artists and writers) are being 'forgotten', who long before the war were very active members of the Communist Party, and the left-wing avant-garde. In addition it is not only persons, but also their Communist persuasion that is being 'forgotten'.

Retention media, connecting the present and the past, also includes historiographies, monuments, memorials and rituals. Ethnography and folklore studies, as well as social anthropology, have 'folk' high on their lists, with its symbolic meaning which is so touchingly looked after by nationalists, communists and, of course, 'Europeans'. Their retention media are countless – conferences, books, magazines, newspapers, films, television series, museum collections, exhibitions, folk music, and dance festivals, and so on. In the Czech Republic there are places and institutions carefully guarding the 'still live traditions' (that would be long defunct without protection) of various anniversary and occasional 'folk festivals'. Some people go as far as to wear 'folk' costumes on these occasions as an expression of their close links with folk traditions and a manifestation of their regional consciousness. Quite frequently these costumes are made according to ethnographic descriptions from the last century or according to museum exhibits.

During the existence of ethnography a number of things have been developed that have played the role of retention media for both nationalism and so-called Marxist social sciences in the countries of 'real socialism'. Today we may witness the shift from the internationalist and class-based interpretation of 'hard data' to interpretations that are either nationalist or 'European'. It is a process analogous to the one that existed in the 1950s only in an opposite or, at least, different direction. Again, 'the present' is conceptualised by using the past, which once again has been reassessed.

The disintegration of the Communist system resulted in the rapid disappearance of a whole system of identities. Generally, this necessitated a search for, or creation of, new identities. Neither the past of an individual, nor that of the whole of society, could simply be negated and so it had, and has to, be 'reassessed'. The creators of the Communist regime proceeded in exactly the same way both initially when they seized power in 1948, and later on during the 'reform' period and after its negation – at the time of so-called normalisation. Today, intellectuals strive to inform the 'present' in such a way as to make it compatible with the longed-for 'European' future. For most people, though, these considerations are too subtle, the topics are so unexciting, that they respond by reverting to well-tried values, such as work, property, family, or even the nation and the state. Some intellectuals express fear at the disruption of moral standards and the deterioration of 'people's' taste. Others such as the pragmatic conservative politicians hold public meetings at Vyšehrad (the legendary seat of the first Czech princes). The insignia of the medieval Czech kings were also exhibited at the inauguration of the first Czech president.

V

The 'present' of far too many post-Communist countries involves 'ethnic' conflicts, or at least tensions expressed in ethnic terms. These have resulted from too radical or, on the contrary, far too slow economic reforms. It is necessary to analyse and explain the war in Bosnia and Herzegovina, the war in Nagorno Karabach, the tensions in Czech–Slovak, or Slovak–Hungarian relations. However, such explanations should be sought not only in the sphere of politics and economy, but also – and perhaps primarily – in the ideological interpretation of cultural differences, and generations-old animosities between 'nations'. Armenian culture, several thousand years old and enriched now by the dominant feature of Christianity, has been put in opposition to the culture of the once nomadic, but primarily Muslim, Azerbaijanis; the enmity between the Czechs and the Germans, invented in the last century, is being revived by left-wing and ultra-right propaganda; Czechoslovakia was depicted as an instrument of the devious Czechs against the genial and naive Slovaks.

The obvious and indisputable fact of language and cultural differences, combining with their political attractiveness, is nowadays presented as something that has existed in the Czech Lands since time immemorial. The present ethnic antagonisms, rooted in economy and politics, are presented as antagonisms of different ethnocultural wholes. This approach is based on the existence of nation-states. This is our current reality – a world divided into a number of nation-states which seemingly and alluringly provide natural conditions for the existence of each one of these wholes. Only these nation-states, it appears, can assure the manifestation of the ethnic and cultural identity of the inhabitants, or at least some of them. Czechoslovakia was finally divided as a result of incompatible economic and political programmes of the victorious political parties. The real basis of the separation, however, is the deep conviction of nationalists that it is necessary to create a nation-state and thereby reach the crowning stage of a nation's development. Once again, we may see the operation of the false assumption that a nation, existing since time immemorial, undergoes development from the nebulous past to the fulfilment of its purpose and goal: the nation-state of the present – and all this in the name of the bright future.

Translated by Aleš Klégr

NOTES

1 Ethnography taken in its 'Central European' sense of a science about the folk of one's nation, rather than the method or subdiscipline of social or cultural anthropology. Perhaps we might even speak of a Central European counterpart to social anthropology, a branch of study called *národopis*

(ethnography and folklore studies in one). This term is due to the different meaning of the concept nation in Czech and in Central Europe in general: a community defined ethnically, culturally, linguistically, historically, politically and, sometimes, even confessionally whose existence precedes the appearance of 'its' nation-state. In the contrary Anglo-Saxon conception the state actually provides the basis for the formation of a nation.

2 *Vlastivěda* (or *Landeskunde* in German) is the cultural history and geography of a country or region with a nationalist, or rather patriotic, interpretation of events and places. In fact it consists in establishing relationships between places (objectively existing in the sense of their physical being) and actions – real or presumed – which occurred in these places in the past. It is a kind of reification of the past in the process of which places in the landscape become the symbol of this past due to specific interpretation. *Vlastivěda* is also a subject taught at elementary schools under all regimes beginning with Austria-Hungary down to the present.

3 Analogous forgeries were made even by Czech Romantic patriots, see also Lass 1988, for further references.

4 On the role of Czech *Volkskunde* in the Czech political movement and on the circumstances of preparations for the 1895 exhibition see Brouček 1979.

5 A considerably more modest exhibition was prepared for 1995–6 as a celebration of the centenary of the 1895 exhibition. It was intended to show the changes in folk's way of life and to present *národopis* (*Volkskunde*) as a discipline which 'still addresses contemporary man'. The spirit of the 1895 exhibition was revived and folk in the sense it was then understood, recalled. The exhibition showed artefacts made by the same folk (i.e. defined in the same way) as once, only a hundred years later. The 'Czechness' as well as the 'folkishness' are axioms, invariable values. The only variable is what this 'Czech folk' produces and what can be used to document the folk's development within the last century. The organiser of this exhibition was the Národopisná společnost ('Ethnographic and Folklore Studies Society') founded originally in connection with preparations for the 1895 exhibition.

6 Such a picture of a peasant, the signs of a 'real' Czech peasant, was treated in Czech fiction and dramatic works of the latter half of the nineteenth century. In this context, we could even agree with A. Robek that literature of this type is an important ethnographic source (Robek 1979). Not, however, for the study of the village of that time, as he recommends, but for the study of the role of ethnography and literature in nation-building processes.

7 Although the independent Czech state disappeared in 1620, the Austrian emperors continued to be crowned Czech kings until 1836. The Czech nationalists never forgave the Emperor Franz Joseph I that he failed to let himself be crowned unlike his predecessors, despite his promises to do so. Priding ourselves on our Czech sense of irony, we should not mind the fact that the last Czech king to be crowned was Ferdinand V the Kind-Hearted, who was forced to abdicate (1848) because of his intellectual insufficiency. He lived until his death (1875) in Prague Castle and reputedly was given, by the citizens of Prague, the friendly nickname *der arme Trottel Nandel* ('the poor idiot Nandel', 'poor' and 'idiot' both in a non-insulting sense) (Galandauer and Honzík 1982).

8 It was a thoroughly nationalist conception for which, in fact, no support could be found in 'the past'. From the early Middle Ages the Czech Lands were settled by an ethnically motley population, from the thirteenth-century colonists from German lands settled here and, after the Thirty Years' War the Czech-speaking population diminished even further. Ideas of an age-long antagonism between both communities began to spread through nationalist propaganda – motivated by economic changes, among other things – only in the nineteenth century. The propaganda mentions incursions of armies from the west (until the twentieth century, however, these were not 'German' armies, but armies from Brandenburg, Passau and Prussia); and German as the language of administration and higher learning is interpreted as an instrument of oppression. The propagandist campaign went as far as to create nationally defined heroes of the Battle of the White Mountain near Prague (8 November 1620), which led to the end of the independent Czech state. These heroes were 'Moravians' who fought to the last. Their Moravian identity implies Czech ethnocultural identity. The textbooks present them as model patriots, determined to fight for their country to the bitter end. This interpretation completely ignores and suppresses the fact that they were mercenaries from the German-speaking pockets in Moravia which casts serious doubt on the Czech nationalist interpretation of their alleged self-sacrifice.

9 I omit here a discussion of the possible uses of retention media, the forms and goals of releasing information (and its selection), of the access to it, of those who guard, release and otherwise control it (and under what conditions); a discussion of the implications of the released, and especially unreleased, information (and of those who control it and the social-political context), the context in which it was received, released or suppressed, touched up, and so on.

10 'To remember' does not mean only 'to store in memory', but primarily to be able to reproduce the things remembered, 'to recall'; retention media are memory, while the interpretation, or evocation (always selective), of their contents is 'remembrance'. On the theory of remembering, see Connerton 1990.

REFERENCES

Anderson, B. (1991) [1983] *Imagined Communities*, London and New York: Verso.

Brouček, S. (1979) *České národopisné hnutí na konci 19. století* ('The Czech Volkskunde Movement at the End of the Nineteenth Century'), Praha: ÚEF ČSAV.

Československá vlastivěda (1968) *Lidová kultura* ('Folk Culture'), Praha: Svoboda.

Connerton, P. (1990) *How Societies Remember*, Cambridge: Cambridge University Press.

Falla, J. (1991) *True Love and Bartholomew: Rebels on the Burmese Border*, Cambridge: Cambridge University Press.

Frolec, V. (1991) 'Etnografické skupiny a moravanství' ('Ethnographic groups and Moravianism'), *Jižní Morava*, 17: 223–58.

Gajek, E. (1990) 'Christmas under the Third Reich', *Anthropology Today* 6(4): 3–9.

Galandauer, J. and Honzík, M. (1982) *Osud trůnu habsburského* ('The Fate of the Hapsburg Throne'), Praha: Panorama.

Gellner, E. (1983) *Nations and Nationalism*, Oxford: Basil Blackwell.

Herder, J. G. (1941) *Vývoj lidskosti* ('Selection from *Ideen* and *Briefe zur Beförderung der Humanität*'), Praha: Jan Laichter.

Hobsbawm, E. J. (1991) *Nations and Nationalism since 1780: Programme, Myth and Reality*, Cambridge: Cambridge University Press.

Hobsbawm, E. J. and Ranger, T. (eds) (1983) *The Invention of Tradition*, Cambridge: Cambridge University Press.

Horák, J. (1933) *Národopis československý: Přehledný nástin* ('Czechoslovak Volkskunde: a brief outline'), *Československá Vlastivěda II – Člověk, Praha: Sfinx, pp. 305–472*.

Hroch, M. (1986) *Evropská národní hnutí v 19. století*, Praha: Svoboda (for an abridged and less biased English version see his *Social Preconditions of National Revival in Europe*, Cambridge: Cambridge University Press, 1985).

Hubinger, V. (1990) 'K vymezení a užití termínu lid v etnografii' ('On the definition and use of the term folk in ethnography'), *Český lid* 77(1): 40–6.

—— (1992) 'Experiencing nationalism: a Central European case', *Folk*, 34: 145–59.

Lass, A. (1988) 'Romantic documents and political monuments: the meaning-fulfillment of history in nineteenth-century Czech nationalism', *American Ethnologist*, 15(3): 456–71.

—— (1989) 'What keeps the Czech folk "Alive"?' *Dialectical Anthropology*, 14: 7–19.

Macura, V. (1992) *Šťastný věk. Symboly, emblémy a mýty 1948–89* ('The Happy Age. Symbols, Emblems and Myths of 1948–89'), Praha: Pražská imaginace.

Národopisná výstava českoslovanská v Praze 1895. Hlavní katalog a průvodce ('The Czechoslavic Ethnographic Exhibition in Prague, 1895: The Main Catalogue and Guide') (1895a) Praha: J. Otto.

Národopisná výstava českoslovanská v Praze 1895 ('Czechoslavic Ethnographic Exhibition in Prague, 1895') (1895b) Praha: J. Otto.

Robek, A. (1979) *Dějiny české etnografie I.* ('History of Czech Ethnography I'), Praha: Státní pedagogické nakladatelství.

Vermeulen, H. F. (1992) *Origins and Institutionalisation of Völkerkunde (1771–1843)*. Paper presented to the Second EASA Conference, Prague (a condensed version appeared as 'The emergence of "ethnography" ca. 1770 in Göttingen', *History of Anthropology Newsletter*, XIX (1992, 2: 6–9).

Chapter 3

The 'Bogoras enigma'
Bounds of cultures and formats of anthropologists

Igor Krupnik

INTRODUCTION

In the spring of 1901, Waldemar Bogoras, the famous Russian anthropologist and a member of the Jesup North Pacific Expedition (1897–1902), surveyed the villages of the Maritime Chukchi and Asiatic Eskimo on the Chukchi Peninsula, Siberia. A few years later the results of his fieldwork appeared in his classic three-volume monograph *The Chukchee* (Bogoras 1904/1909), published in the Jesup Expedition series, under the general editorship of Franz Boas. In describing the social system of the native people he studied, Bogoras claimed that their coastal village was nothing but a territorial unit and did not have 'any organization beyond the fact that the inhabitants are neighbors and are friendly among themselves' (Bogoras 1904/1909: 544). Some twenty-five years later he reaffirmed the same statement in another publication: 'The maritime villages, even the largest of them, have no inner organization and are governed by no one, beyond the custom and the public opinion' (Bogoras 1930: 70).

By this assertion Bogoras imposed some sort of anthropological 'bounds' upon social reality he observed, even in a negative way. But the patriarch of Siberian ethnography proved to be wrong. Coastal communities of both the Eskimo and Maritime Chukchi *did* possess a social structure of their own, and one of a very complex type. Due to Bogoras's indisputable reputation it was not revealed by successive students but only many decades later: first for the Asiatic Eskimo (Chlenov 1973; Krupnik and Chlenov 1979; Menovshchikov 1962; Sergeev 1962; Shnakenburg 1939), and then for the Chukchi (Leont'ev 1972; Vdovin 1965). An Eskimo village turned out to be a social entity of several clans and clan-based neighbourhoods bound by kin ties, marital preferences, land and ritual regulations, struggle for prestige, and so on. Larger communities were also divided into opposing territorial moieties, with a textbook set of anthropological riches – conflicts and rivalries, personal names and pejorative nicknames, athletic competitions, ball games, and so on (Chlenov and Krupnik 1995; Krupnik 1991).

The key challenge of the 'Bogoras enigma' – as I call it throughout this text – is evident. Bogoras was not a missionary, naval explorer, or an armchair evolutionist, but a skilled field ethnographer in a truly modern sense. Due to his outstanding experience and time spent in the field, he was fluent in local languages, and capable in depicting even the slightest details of native culture. And it was he who surprisingly missed the very social cornerstone of the native people with whom he lived for several months.

THE EXPLANATORY MODELS

A misinterpretation or misjudgement by a fieldworker of Bogoras's stature is by far an instructive phenomenon in itself. As such, it may be a useful key to revealing some sources of anthropological biases in interpreting the 'wholes' of other cultures. I'll use this issue as a case study for my perspective on how field anthropologists impose bounds on ethnographic reality they watch, and from where the difference begins between what they write and what they actually observe.

A thriving plethora of Eskimo social life must have been fully open to Bogoras's observation, and is actually portrayed in fragments throughout his voluminous publications. In my own field accounts, seventy-five years after Bogoras's visit, that system was still within the reach of anthropological study. Though extinct by the 1940s as a viable network, due to Soviet pressure and acculturation, it was found to be readily recountable through the memories of older people. Vivid stories were recorded from numerous informants on former social structures that had regulated the life style of their grandparents once queried by the famous ethnographer. In the very same Eskimo village where Bogoras had lived for about two months, seventy years later elders easily listed the names of clans and neighborhoods of the early 1900s. None of these names was ever mentioned in volumes of Bogoras's Eskimo and Chukchi publications.

There are a number of options to consider with regard to this striking incongruity in the accounts presented by Bogoras *vis-à-vis* those of later anthropologists and of the existing native tradition. The easiest explanation derives from the general advancement of anthropology as a discipline. With the available database on the variety of human social systems, no modern student would ever dare to claim a native community could exist *without* a social organisation, just an aggregation of people 'who are nothing but friendly to each other'.

The accumulated legacy of anthropology, as such, might act as the driving factor that forced later fieldworkers to be more persistent and/or more sophisticated in the search for specific social institutions of the cultures they studied. One could even say that anthropologists eventually became too much obsessed with choosing among the conflicting patterns of social structures to be used as models. The debates of the 1960s and 1970s on whether the Asiatic Eskimo kin groups were formerly exogamous *gentes* or endogamous clans (see Chlenov 1973) serve as a good illustration. That problem Bogoras seemingly did not face at all.

Second, one may look for cultural transformation. It is easy to assume that the Eskimo society described by Bogoras has been profoundly changed by the time of later accounts. Over the decades of contacts and acculturation, some of the social institutions might have become more apparent or simply preserved as single survivors of the former system that had undergone changes. That might explain why later students are eager to record a social network that was low profile or did not exist in Bogoras's time.

We can examine this statement, at least for the same Asiatic Eskimo village of Ungazik where Bogoras stayed for two months in April–June of 1901 and where he found 'no inner organization'. To our advantage, he made a village family census which is included in his field diary (Bogoras 1901). Though Bogoras obviously never made any use of this list, we used it with Michael Chlenov to interview the local elders in 1981 (Chlenov and Krupnik 1995). All of them were born *after* 1901, that is after Bogoras's census. Nevertheless, the elders easily identified the majority of families recorded in Bogoras's list and arranged them according to clan and neighbourhood affiliation. Some of the reported people were their parents or elder relatives, and the informants had no trouble reciting their position within the former social network. Hence, there are sufficient grounds for expecting continuity in social structures unrecorded by Bogoras, instead of modelling a new system that supposedly has 'surfaced' through later transformation.

Yet another explanation might be that we are dealing with an incorrect statement or an observational failure somehow stemming from Bogoras's field practices. If so, the story turns out to be a case of professional misjudgement. But before pointing a finger at the founder of Siberian ethnography for his failure to record a social system he observed, we have to examine the ways anthropology was done in the area in Bogoras's time.

ORIGIN OF BIASES: A PRESENT-DAY INVENTORY

Field ethnography in northeast Siberia in 1900 differed greatly from the style that Franz Boas, Bogoras's supervisor and organiser of the Jesup North Pacific Expedition, made use of on the American Northwest Coast as a part of the same Jesup programme. Though Boas is rightly credited with introducing field ethnography as a key component of modern anthropology, his own major field practice was that of brief summer visits ('flying visits'). After his year-long Baffinland expedition of 1883–84, he rarely spent more than a few months in most of the places he visited (Stocking 1974: 83–6; Van Maanen 1988: 36). Hard as fieldwork and transportation through the wilderness of British Columbia may have been in the 1890s and 1900s (see Boas 1898; Rohner 1969), it took place at the close margins of expanding industrial civilisation. Boas normally arrived in the field by train from New York and was rarely, if ever, in long isolation from telegraph, post office, bank and local steamer.

For Bogoras and for other members of the Jesup Expedition who worked in northeast Siberia, the situation was quite different. As Bogoras reported in a letter to Boas:

> My long journey from the mouth of the Anadyr River through the Gizhiga district to Kamchatka and a long way along the sea coast to Anadyr took me five months. During that time I made 4000 miles with dogs. A considerable part of my way was not made till now by any civilized man. Our journey went through an unpeopled country, where we could not find any guide and had to find our way, being guided by the sun and following the rivers. I returned in a very poor state of health. There were a few days when I almost thought I will not be able to reach Anadyr at all.
>
> (Bogoras to Boas, 1901)

Bogoras, however, was well equipped for his mission by eight previous years he spent in Siberia, as a political exile. Though lacking an anthropological education, he had extensive fieldwork experience, due to his participation in the Yakutian Expedition of 1895–7 sponsored by Russian philanthropist, Ivan Sibiriakov, and in the First Russian National Census of 1897. He got intimate knowledge of natives and native languages of Arctic Siberia, and contributed several papers on local ethnography and folklore before the Jesup field trip of 1900–1. Bogoras seemingly received extensive orientation from Boas prior to going to Siberia and during the subsequent years when he worked on his field materials in New York (1902–4). Thus, in certain respects, we may well consider him a trained and mature professional sent for a year-long project under a programme designed by his academic supervisor.

From that point of view, Bogoras made a truly outstanding contribution to the Jesup Expedition programme and to Siberian anthropology in general. As Boas quoted Bogoras's final report:

The results of this work are studies of the ethnography and anthropology of the Chukchee and Asiatic Eskimo, and partly of the Kamchadal and of the Pacific Koryak. These studies are illustrated by extensive collections, embracing five thousand ethnographical objects, thirty three plaster casts of faces, seventy-five skulls and archaeological specimens from abandoned village sites and from graves. Other material obtained includes three hundred tales and traditions; one hundred fifty texts in the Chukchee, Koryak, Kamchadal and Eskimo languages; dictionaries and grammatical sketches of these languages; ninety-five phonographic records, and measurements of eight hundred sixty individuals [the latter done mainly by Bogoras' companion, Mr Axelrod – I.K.]. I also made a zoological collection and kept a meteorological journal during the whole time of my field-work.

(Boas 1903:115)

Bogoras's work for the Jesup Expedition resulted in eight monographs: a three-volume ethnography of the Chukchi, a volume of Chukchi mythology, and four volumes on folklore and languages of other local nations (Bogoras 1904/1909, 1910, 1913, 1917, 1918, 1949). Various materials were also presented in scores of other publications (see Vinnikov 1935). According to one recent evaluation, 'no modern anthropologist has ever collected such a diversity of data' (Freed, Freed and Williamson 1988: 20).

But there existed, I imagine, some intrinsic blockages in his programme of which any modern anthropologist going to the field is quite aware. Carrying out my own field studies in the same area of Siberia, I could well appreciate both the problems Bogoras faced and his remarkable achievements.

During the fieldwork, time and energy expenditures on the logistics of settling and transportation were gruelling. For the entire calendar year Bogoras spent in Siberia (August 1900–July 1901), he was mainly on the move, travelling by dog- and reindeer sledges, and skin boats. Within that year he surveyed an area from the Bering Strait to Kamchatka Peninsula, over a distance equal to a round trip from London to Sicily, or from the Arctic Coast of North America to British Columbia.

At age of 35, he suffered from enormous physical hardships on his routes and actually was ill during a part and very soon after his fieldwork. As he reported to Boas:

> I was taken ill with influenza in one of the Kamchatka villages and lost my voice temporarily, so that I could communicate with the natives only by means of signs during more than a fortnight. At one time, indeed, my illness became so alarming that the Cossack [his companion, I.K.] asked me for instructions as to which way to carry my body and my 'official papers' in case I should die on the route.
> (Boas 1903: 114)

His complete physical recovery took several months after he finally arrived in St Petersburg. For more than half a year after that Bogoras was unable to travel to New York and even to stand much physical exercise (Kuz'mina 1993). Actually, Bogoras never returned to the field after 1901 and the only way he could update his materials was to send his younger students some twenty-five years later.

As modern fieldworkers, we can also appreciate his labour and intellectual investment in the academic content of his programme. Bogoras's main goal was to make ethnographic collections for the American Museum of Natural History in New York. Beyond this major focus, he also studied native folklore and languages, took photographs and anthropological measurements, recorded vocabularies and folklore texts in notebooks and on the phonograph cylinders. That was the way 'basic ethnographies' were prepared in the early 1900s. As Boas pointed out in his guidelines to Waldemar Jochelson, Bogoras's companion and official leader of the Jesup Siberian team:

> The scope of your work among the Koryak and the Yukagheer would be the following. You would have to make collections of specimens illustrating the customs and the physical characteristics of the people. These collections should include ethnological specimens of all kinds, – skeletons and skulls, so far as these can be obtained, photographs, and casts in plaster-of-paris. Your studies would be

devoted primarily to the ethnology of the people, including a thorough study of language and mythology and anthropometric measures.

(Boas to Jochelson, 28 October 1898)

It was not the too wide focus of the field survey, but rather the 'double-message' imposed on Bogoras by Boas, the expedition's scientific supervisor, that might have acted as an additional source of frustration. The Jesup North Pacific Expedition was launched to study whether human affinities on the Siberian and American sides of the Pacific are due to mixture, to early migrations, or to gradual cultural differentiation (Boas 1898: 6; 1903: 74). Despite its rather broadly declared goal, the expedition was an academic project, in a fairly modern sense. It had a specific focus on a number of selected research strategies, first and foremost on recording native folklore and languages, analysing certain cultural features (such as basketry or facial paintings), making anthropometric surveys of the local populations, and so on.

Boas's ideas on the role of each of his subordinates who went to the field were never presented explicitly for modern re-evaluation. But Boas apparently had some sort of 'double-views' for the Siberian and American contributions to the joint programme. The American team could rely on the previous basic ethnographies available for the larger part of its study area and/or on the earlier data collected by Boas himself (e.g. Boas 1890, 1891, 1897; Eells 1889; Niblack 1890 – see Boas 1903: 77; Suttles and Jonaitis 1990: 73–5). Hence, the American team had a free hand to concentrate on some specific research tasks for the sake of future comparative studies which, in fact, the Americans never fulfilled.

The Russian team, on the other hand, of which Bogoras was a member, had to do both 'basic ethnographies' *and* gathering of linguistic, folkloric, and other data to prove prehistoric Siberian–American connections, *and* collection of ethnographic museum specimens as well. These three tasks blend poorly in any modern field research for they require different orientations and logistics of one's field strategy.

I would argue that it was more or less the same for Bogoras in 1900. The Russian participants realised it long before they had to go to the field, and they tried to split the functions by creating a joint team:

It would be much more advisable to make a greater part of it [fieldwork, I.K.] together and to change consequently in some aspects the distribution of work, as was settled before. [. . .] Besides that we think that generally the division of work in the time of journey will be of great utility, whereas the single traveller must in the same time undertake too much different things, and it is to be feared, he could not be very close in attending them all. [. . .] Mr. Jochelson takes upon himself specially photographs, anthropological measurements, and making of masks. My separate share shall be, as I told before, the study of language. Ethnographic study shall be made by both.

(Bogoras and Jochelson to Boas, 30 October 1899)

Unfortunately, for some unknown reasons, that scenario did not materialise.

The blend of comparative, museum, and general descriptive commitments was only a part of the logistical burden placed on the Russian team. Both Bogoras and Jochelson apparently had their personal 'hidden agendas' within the Jesup programme, as they were anxious to expand their previous fieldwork in Siberia with a new broader survey. This created a situation in which the Russian participants had to study *several* ethnic groups within one extended field season. Thus, they became *comparative* ethnographers from the very beginning. Boas did his best to stop this trend:

The principal object of your work [of both Jochelson and Bogoras, I.K.] will be a thorough investigation of the Koryak, maritime Chukchee, and eastern Yukagheer from all points of view, ethnological, linguistical, and somatological. [. . .] You will make studies and collections among the Lamoot, reindeer Chukchee, Eskimo, and Kamchadal if opportunity should offer; but these are not the primary object of the expedition.

(Boas to Jochelson, 26 March 1900)

He failed, however, in this regard. Both Jochelson and Bogoras have far extended the range of their fieldwork beyond their original assignments. In addition to so-called 'principal objects', they also surveyed *all* the groups mentioned in Boas's 'secondary' list and even several others (e.g. Yakut, Russian Creoles, Kerek, St Lawrence Island Eskimo, western Yukaghir). As one could expect, it provided much new and truly unique data, but also caused many additional troubles.

Bogoras reached the Maritime Chukchi (his primary study group, according to Boas's assignment) and Asiatic Eskimo only in the spring of 1901, after he spent two months among the Koryak, two months among the Itelmen, and several weeks among the Russian Creoles. His basic and most extensive anthropological knowledge, however, was obtained while studying the Reindeer Chukchi in the mid-1890s (1895–97). Bogoras preserved his Chukchi devotion throughout his whole academic career and through the Jesup fieldwork as well. Actually, he looked at other Siberian native nations from the perspective of his Reindeer Chukchi experience, a fact which is underlined by several explicit remarks in his three-volume Jesup monograph.

By virtue of their craft, anthropologists claim to be objective and relativistic. But normally they 'favour' some of the people they study, share their attitudes towards neighbours, and add numerous personal arguments to ground such a favouritism. This pattern is well known to any modern student who has surveyed more than one group in the course of his or her professional career. Bogoras, the devoted disciple of reindeer people, did the same in 1901, when he settled in the maritime Eskimo village for extensive fieldwork. While staying there, he routinely used his impeccable command of the Chukchi language for communicating with his Eskimo informants. He simply came from *another* native culture and placed its bounds and perspective on the new reality. By that strategy, he eventually opened the door to certain limitations and misunderstandings.

WRITING THE 'CULTURAL WHOLES'

We could similarly derive a number of other explanations to place Bogoras's field practices under modern scrutiny. My focus, however, is not on displaying potential grounds for error some 90 years old, but to understand the sources for our present biases in interpreting cultures we study. Bogoras's example is extremely helpful in this respect.

From its very inception, anthropology is a controversial discipline. Its main goal, to impose the bounds of typology and structure on the thriving variety of humankind, is pretentious, by definition. Its major method, fieldwork, is hypocritical in its focus on investigator's mimicry and elaborate techniques that permit entering and observing alien cultures, otherwise closed to the outsider. The discord between those two missions is quite a source of personal tension. Sometimes it also serves as a powerful tool to spur the development of our science.

That intrinsic ambiguity of anthropology overlaps with its general obsession shared by all positivistic social sciences and by modern scholarship in general. If the specific goal of anthropology is to be postulated, it would be one of diminishing entropy of unclassified facts in human cultural variety. Normally, this task is addressed by placing organising bounds on the 'unbounded reality', in the form of theories, typologies, models, observed and recorded phenomena, and so on.

Being an established academic discipline for some 150 years, anthropology has accumulated an enormous stockpile of previous intellectual efforts. Hence, its modern history is mainly a chronicle of the refutation of preceding theoretical and empirical assumptions, that is, of re-bounding, reshaping of a previously structuralised reality captured elsewhere from the 'unbounded chaos'. Although we commonly share a holistic view of culture, as of a somehow integrated whole, we are in fact juggling with various paradigms of that whole produced by numerous competing doctrines. Some people take it seriously, others not; a few rebel.

The rebels normally wave the banners of 'cultural boundlessness' in their dissent against the domination of the 'bounding speculativeness'. Franz Boas, Bogoras's field supervisor and himself a staunch opponent of any rigid theoretical bounds placed over the variety of human cultures, expressed it quite explicitly in one of his early attacks against what he called introducing 'the rigid abstractions species, genus, and family into ethnology, the true meaning of which it took so long to understand' (Boas 1887; see: Stocking 1974: 62). Some thirty years later Boas repeated his stand in an even stronger form when he said that 'We refrain from the attempt to solve the fundamental problem of the general development of civilization until we have been able to unravel the processes that are going on under our eyes' (Boas 1940: 285). Therefore, a general trend to expand the area of 'bounded', that is, of firmly classified and neatly tied phenomena, is dotted with mighty 'resistentialist' doctrines, be it Boasian 'historical method', post-modernism, or any other form of cultural relativism.

As attractive as it might be, it is hard to expel 'bounds' from the discipline altogether. Modern anthropologists are strong in advocating their craft as 'writing cultures', 'reading cultures', or even 'translating cultures' (Clifford 1986; Asad 1986; Palsson 1992). Those are fairly general labels that actually embrace several distinctive steps in anthropological enterprise. Using modern language, we may entitle these steps as *visioning culture*, *processing culture*, and *formatting culture*, before *textualising* its whole in a final, that is, textual form.

Though visioning of an alien life seems quite an 'unbounded' process, it obviously has its own limitations based on the training and personality of the observer, and the tolerance of the observed. (One could argue that 'visioning' is not just 'looking', but any form of sensorial experience as well as recording and inquiring about the phenomena perceived.) To overcome those limitations, anthropology has developed numerous *processing* methods to ensure decoding of the non-visual cultural components. Genealogies, village censuses, maps, kinship systems, network charts, graphic and projective testings, historical records, sociological questionnaires, componential analysis, and several other research techniques are routine modern tools accumulated through decades of fieldwork experience. *Formatting* is then the way anthropologists organise the 'whole' of culture into a set of inner structural blocks and place those blocks in a certain logical order throughout their studies. The final writing (*textualising*) presents an entirely sovereign intellectual endeavour following regulations and principles of its own (Marcus 1986). As such, there are numerous options for placing deliberate or inherent bounds on initial reality at each succeeding step.

Progress in the discipline eventually elaborates all four (and several other) components of anthropological process. It goes neither evenly nor simultaneously along the field's frontline. Although our technical abilities to visualise cultures have improved dramatically (due to video, tape-recording, colour-slide photography, etc.), we are not far ahead, if not behind our predecessors in skill of observation. We are definitely inferior in *textualising* cultures, as it is hard to find any modern worker capable of publishing eight volumes from one field season (as Bogoras did). Our major strengths, I suppose, are in the realm of *processing* non-visual facets of culture, such as social structures, kin relationships, economy and politics, psychological motives of human behaviour and interactions, encoded symbolism, invisible traces of earlier stages, and so on.

That last drift caused a revolutionary transition in the way we *format* 'cultural wholes' nowadays. Compared to Boas and Bogoras's time, we have made a dramatic shift in anthropological focus from material culture and folklore to social reality and human interactions. No one today would start a modern anthropological monograph with a section on clothing, garments or facial paintings, that is, with the most *visual* signs of otherness, that was typical for an ethnography of the late 1800s. We are, thus, formatting cultures in different inner moulds, placing new accents on each of them, and finally binding them under a novel pagination, while writing our texts.

FORMATTING THE FIELDWORK EXPERIENCE:
BOGORAS AND BOAS

Now we have enough general theory to return to the enigma of Bogoras. Though a trained and earnest student, he overscheduled his time in the field in favour of travelling as opposed to a more stationary observation and data-collecting. The programme set by his supervisor was too profuse and based on numerous conflicting commitments. The fieldworker was biased by his previous experience and deep devotion to a certain group of native people whom he knew better and ranked higher than others. Those are major bounds of Bogoras's cultural 'visioning', quite familiar to any modern student who ever experienced similar imbalances in field programme.

And finally, when Bogoras came back from the field burgeoned with new data and original ideas, he was persuaded by Boas to adopt Boasian pattern of cultural 'formatting' for his final writings. The format Boas tried to ensure throughout the Jesup Expedition volumes, was that of a 'basic ethnography'. By modern standards, it was an ambitiously detailed handbook of a native nation covering its every aspect, from habitat, physical appearance and stone lamps to social rites, religion and mythology.

Boas himself experimented with this pattern for the first time in 1888, in his monograph on the Central Eskimo (Boas 1888). By the 1890s however, it surfaced as an established, if not official format in North American Arctic ethnography (cf. Murdoch 1888; Turner 1894; Nelson 1899; Boas 1901). That fact Boas definitely had in mind when designing the Jesup North Pacific Expedition series. At least seven of its volumes (Boas 1909; Bogoras 1904/1909; Jochelson 1908, 1926; Teit 1900, 1906, 1909) follow that same pattern pioneered by Boas and Murdoch in the 1880s, with only one – that of Swanton on the Haida (Swanton 1905) – being different, due to its noticeable focus on native social structures and genealogies.

From a modern point of view, a Boasian 'basic ethnography' was too much a museum display blend of technology, spiritual beliefs and folklore. But it certainly was the dominant way anthropologists formatted native cultures at the turn of the century. In Arctic studies that pattern survived well into the 1920s. It was subsequently replicated by several later 'basic monographs' produced by the next generation of Arctic researchers (Birket-Smith 1924; 1929; Mathiassen 1928; Thalbitzer 1914–41).

It was obvious that Boas had deliberately adopted that format to encompass the 'whole' of North Pacific native cultures, due to the primarily museum focus of the Jesup Expedition. I would guess that his idea was to create, through Jesup publications, a full 'handbook' series for the entire North Pacific area, with the 'Russian' (Siberian) volumes fitting the dominant pattern on the American side. One could argue, however, that his previous field experience and his personal view of the cultural 'holism' played an important role in that choice as well. Boasian holism was first and foremost influenced by strong emphasis on text and myth as a core of anthropological endeavour and the best projection/integration of the 'genius of peoples' (Stocking 1974: 4–8, 86). That explains why *all* Jesup volumes have large sections of folklore texts, and particularly of myths. The trick is that the 'material culture-and-myth' combination advocated by Boas, was neither the only nor probably the best pattern of cultural 'formatting' available at that time.

During the same decade of 1897–1907 marked by major Jesup fieldwork and publications, the British Cambridge Anthropological Expedition under Prof. Alfred Cort Haddon produced its six-volume synthesis of the culture of the Torres Straits natives based on a six-month survey in 1898. Unlike the Jesup volumes, the Cambridge series is far more focused on social systems and regional synopses and has much better balance (at least, from my perspective) between native material life, spiritual beliefs and social organisation. It burgeoned with an amazing amount of local details: names of clans, other social fragments, local chiefs, and so on (Haddon 1904, 1908). It also made much better use of village censuses, local tribal maps, genealogies, clan histories, and other 'non-visual' stuff to be used in data-collecting and further processing. Rivers, for example, utilised his genealogies and village lists to calculate shares of various family and marriage patterns (Rivers 1904), more or less in the same manner we processed Bogoras's Eskimo village census of 1901 in the 1980s. That form of processing was never done by Bogoras himself.

As a result, the Cambridge team introduced an entirely different pattern of ethnographic handbook and succeeded in 'textualising culture' under a far more influential format than any of the Jesup monographs. The divergence became even more obvious in the next generation of the two respective traditions – if one picks as examples *The Andaman Islanders* of Radcliffe-Brown (1922) and Birket-Smith's 'Ethnology of the Egedesminde District' (1924). I wonder whether Boas and other Jesup participants ever got a chance to acknowledge that fact.

Conflicting personal roles and preferences may have influenced

Bogoras–Boas relationships as much as they do elsewhere today. Bogoras, as he proved through his later academic career, tended to be speculative and open to hierarchical evolutionism, particularly in the field of native religion, mentality and prehistoric cultural connections (Bogoras 1906, 1925, 1929). He even succeeded in 'smuggling' some of his evolutionist ideas on the origin of primitive religion into his Chukchi monograph in the Jesup series (Bogoras 1904/1909: 277–80; Kan 1992: 11). Boas, on the other hand, was a true anti-evolutionist who tried to eliminate any sources of theoretical speculations in 'bounding' variety of native cultures through the Jesup publications. After all, as Sergei Kan notes, Boas had hired Bogoras and others to collect data for Siberian ethnographies and not to engage in speculations (Kan 1992: 8).

As a supervisor of a multi-volume project, it was Boas who designed hierarchical research niches for every participant and required Bogoras to observe the format of a museum-display handbook for his Chukchi and Eskimo field data. Under that format of a 'basic ethnography', the gaps and biases of Bogoras' vision of native cultures became evident. While chapters on clothing, housing, subsistence implements, *and* ceremonials in his monograph *The Chukchee* are more or less equally balanced between the Reindeer and Maritime brand, those on social life are surprisingly assymmetric. There is, for example, a forty-page description of marriage patterns among the reindeer people counter-balanced by hardly three pages devoted to the same subject for the coastal folk. Hence the 'Bogoras enigma', a portrait of a coastal village whose residents are nothing but neighbours 'friendly among themselves', appeared as a result.

SUMMARY

The above mentioned controversy is by no means a prerogative of a century-old Arctic expedition or of any research in traditional societies with conflicting roles imposed by the personal preferences and commitments of the investigators. Arrogance in bounding other cultures at each stage of anthropological pursuit – be it visioning, processing, formatting or textualising – is an original sin of anthropology, as a discipline. Every new student in the field has to pass through the same test, and patterns of providing feedback developed by generations of professionals prove to be of limited value.

The main dichotomy within the science of anthropology still exists, as it did in the time of Bogoras. It is focused on our individual response to the major question of the discipline. Whether we have to proceed in 'formatting' the wholes of other cultures or just in 'mirroring' their fluid and never bounded faces, is a matter of our personal choice. Each generation of anthropologists faces the same challenge of the inconsistency between previously accumulated formatting theories and the electrifying harvest of individual fieldwork. As such, the contrast between the pluralism of communally shared knowledge and the arrogance of personal experience remains unsolved.

REFERENCES

Asad, Talal (1986) 'The concept of cultural translation in British social anthropology', in J. Clifford and G. Marcus (eds), *Writing Culture: The Poetics and Politics of Ethnography*, Berkeley and Los Angeles: University of California Press, pp. 141–64.

Birket-Smith, Kai (1924) 'Ethnography of the Egedesminde District, with aspects of the general culture of West Greenland', *Meddelelser om Gronland* 66, Copenhagen.

—— (1929) *The Caribou Eskimos; Material and Social Life and Their Cultural Position*, Report of the Fifth Thule Expedition 1921–1924, vol. 5, parts 1–2, Copenhagen.

Boas, Franz (1887) 'The occurrence of similar inventions in areas widely apart', *Science*, 9: 485–6.

—— (1888) 'The Central Eskimo', *Sixth Annual Report of the Bureau of American Ethnology*, Washington, pp. 399–669; repr. Lincoln, Nebr.: The University of Nebraska Press, 1964.

—— (1890) 'First general report on the Indians of British Columbia (Tlingit, Haida, Tsimshian, Kutonaga)', *Report of the British Association for the Advancement of Science*, 59, London: pp. 801–93.

—— (1891) 'Second general report on the Indians of British Columbia', in *Report of the British Association for the Advancement of Science*, 60, London, pp. 562–715.

—— (1897) 'The social organization and the secret societies of the Kwakiutl Indians', *Report of the U.S. National Museum for 1895*: Washington, pp. 311–738.

—— (1898) 'The Jesup North Pacific Expedition: introduction', *The Jesup North Pacific Expedition*, vol. 1, part 1: 3–11; repr. New York: AMS Press, 1975.

—— (1901) 'The Eskimo of Baffin Land and Hudson Bay', *Bulletin of the American Museum of Natural History*, 15: 1–370.

—— (1903) 'The Jesup North Pacific Expedition', *The American Museum Journal* 3(5): 73–119.

—— (1909) 'The Kwakiutl of the Vancouver Island', *The Jesup North Pacific Expedition*, vol. 5, part 2: 301–522; repr. New York: AMS Press, 1975.

—— (1940) *Race, Language and Culture*, New York: Macmillan Company.

Bogoras, Waldemar (1901) 'Dnevnik vo vremya puteshestviia i prebyvaniia v Unyine', Archive of the Russian Academy of Sciences, St Petersburg, F.250, Book 1, No. 116.

—— (1904/1909) The Chukchee: Material culture, Religion, Social Organization, 3 vols, The Jesup North Pacific Expedition, vol. 7, parts 1–3; repr. New
York: AMS Press, 1975.
—— (1906) 'Religious ideas of primitive man, from Chukchee material',
Internationaler Americanisten-Kongress, XIV: 129–35.
—— (1910) Chukchee Mythology, The Jesup North Pacific Expedition, vol. 8,
part 1, pp. 1–197; repr. New York: AMS Press, 1975.
—— (1913) The Eskimo of Siberia, The Jesup North Pacific Expedition, vol. 8,
part 3, pp. 417–56; repr. New York: AMS Press, 1975.
—— (1917) 'Koryak Texts', Publications of the American Ethnological Society,
vol. V, Leiden.
—— (1918) 'Tales of Yukaghir, Lamut, and Russianized natives of Eastern
Siberia', Anthropological Papers of the American Museum of Natural
History, 20(1): 3–148.
—— (1925) 'Ideas of space and time in the conception of primitive religion',
American Anthropologist, 27(2): 205–66.
—— (1929) 'Elements of the culture of the circumpolar zone', American
Anthropologist, 31(4): 579–601.
—— (1930) 'Chukotskii obshchestvennyi stroi po dannym fol'klora', Sovetskii
Sever, 6: 63–79.
—— (1949) Materialy po iazyku aziatskikh eskimosov, Leningrad: Uchpedgiz.
Chlenov, Michael (1973) 'Distinctive features of the social organization of the
Asiatic Eskimos', paper submitted to the IXth International Congress of
Anthropological and Ethnological Science, Institute of Ethnography: Moscow.
Chlenov, Michael and Krupnik, Igor (1995) Survival in Contact: Asiatic Eskimo
Transitions, 1900–1990, Washington, DC: Smithsonian Institution Press.
Clifford, James (1986) 'Introduction: partial truths', in J. Clifford and G.
Marcus (eds), Writing Culture: The Poetics and Politics of Ethnography,
Berkeley and Los Angeles: University of California Press, pp. 1–26.
Eells, Myron (1889) 'The Twana, Chemakum, and Klallam Indians of
Washington Territory', Annual Report of the Smithsonian Institution for
the Year 1887, Washington, DC: Smithsonian Institute, pp. 605–81.
Freed, Stanley A., Freed, Ruth S. and Williamson, Laila (1988) 'Capitalist
philanthropy and Russian revolutionaries: the Jesup North Pacific Expedi-
tion', American Anthropologist, 90(1): 7–24.
Haddon, Alfred Cort (ed.) (1904) Sociology, Magic and Religion of the Western
Islanders, Reports of the Cambridge Anthropological Expedition to Torres
Strait, vol. 5, Cambridge: Cambridge University Press.
—— (ed.) (1908) Sociology, Magic and Religion of the Eastern Islanders,
Reports of The Cambridge Anthropological Expedition to Torres Strait, vol.
6, Cambridge: Cambridge University Press.
Jochelson, Waldemar (1908) The Koryak, The Jesup North Pacific Expedition,
vol. 6, parts 1–2; repr. New York: AMS Press, 1975.
—— (1926) The Yukaghir and Yukaghized Tungus, The Jesup North Pacific
Expedition, vol. 9, parts 1–3; repr. New York: AMS Press, 1975.
Kan, Sergei (1992) 'Boas' research agenda and the Russian participants in the
Jesup Expedition', Paper delivered at the First International Congress of
Arctic Social Sciences, 29 October, Quebec, Canada (quoted with author's
permission).

Krupnik, Igor (1991) 'Fêtes hivernales "privées" chez les Eskimos asiatiques', *Etudes/Inuit/Studies*, 14(1–2): 159–68.

Krupnik, Igor and Chlenov, Mikhail (1979) 'Dinamika etnolingvisticheskoi situatsii u aziatskikh eskimosov (konets XIX v. –1970e gody)', *Sovetskaia etnografiia*, 2: 19–29.

Kuz'mina, Liudmila P. (1993) 'The Jesup North Pacific Expedition (from the History of Russian–American Cooperation', in W. Fitzhugh and V. Chaussonnet (eds), *Anthropology of the North Pacific Rim*, Washington, DC: Smithsonian Institution Press.

Leont'ev Vladilen V. (1972) 'Etnicheskaia istoria poselka Uelen', *Kraevedcheskie zapiski*, 9: 83–93.

Marcus, George E. (1986) 'Afterword: ethnographic writing and anthropological careers', in J. Clifford and G. Marcus (eds), *Writing Culture. The Poetics and Politics of Ethnography*, Berkeley and Los Angeles: University of California Press, pp. 262–6.

Mathiassen, Therkel (1928) *Material Culture of the Iglulik Eskimos*, Report of the Fifth Thule Expedition 1921–1924, vol. 6, part 1, Copenhagen.

Menovshchikov, Georgii A. (1962) 'O perezhitochnykh yavleniyakh rodovoi organisatsii u aziatskikh eskimosov', *Sovetskaia etnografiia*, 6: 29–34.

Murdoch, John (1888) 'Ethnological results of the Point Barrow Expedition', *9th Annual Report of the Bureau of American Ethnology for the Years 1887–1888*, pp. 3–441; repr. Washington, DC: Smithsonian Institution Press, 1988.

Nelson, Edward W. (1899) 'The Eskimo about Bering Strait', *18th Annual Report of the Bureau of American Ethnology for the Years 1896–1897*, pp. 3–518; repr. Washington DC: Smithsonian Institution Press, 1983.

Niblack, Charles G. (1890) 'The coast Indians of southern Alaska and northern British Columbia', *Annual Report of the U.S. National Museum for 1888*, pp. 225–386.

Palsson, Gisli (ed.) (1992) *Beyond Boundaries: Understanding, Translation and Anthropological Discourse*, Leamington: Berg Publishers.

Radcliffe-Brown, Alfred R. (1922) *The Andaman Islanders*, Cambridge: Cambridge University Press.

Rivers, Willaim Halse (1904) 'Genealogies. Regulation of marriage', *Reports of the Cambridge Anthropological Expedition to Torres Straits*, vol. 5, Cambridge: Cambridge University Press, pp. 122–8, 233–47.

Rohner, Ronald (ed.) (1969) *The Ethnography of Franz Boas*, Chicago: University of Chicago Press.

Sergeev, Dorian A. (1962) 'Perezhitki otsovskogo roda u aziatskikh eskimosov', *Sovetskaia etnografiia*, 6: 35–42.

Shnakenburg, Nikolai B. (1939) 'Eskimosy', manuscript, Archive of the Institute-Museum of Ethnography and Anthropology, F.K-I, Op. 1, no. 557. St Petersburg.

Stocking, George W., Jr (1974) *The Shaping of American Anthropology 1883–1911: A Franz Boas Reader*. New York: Basic Books.

Suttles, Wayne and Jonaitis, Aldona C. (1990) 'History of research in ethnology', in W. Suttles (ed.), *Northwest Coast: Handbook of North American Indians*, vol. 7, Washington: Smithsonian Institution, pp. 73–87.

Swanton, John R. (1905) *Contributions to the Ethnology of the Haida*, The

Jesup North Pacific Expedition, vol. 5, part 1, pp. 1–300; repr. New York: AMS Press, 1975.

Teit, James Alexander (1900) *The Thompson Indians of British Columbia*, The Jesup North Pacific Expedition, vol. 1, part 4, pp. 163–392; repr. New York: AMS Press, 1975.

—— (1906) *The Lillooet Indians*, The Jesup North Pacific Expedition, vol. 2, part 5, pp. 192–300; repr. New York: AMS Press, 1975.

—— (1909) *The Shuswap*, The Jesup North Pacific Expedition, vol. 2, part 7, pp. 443–813; repr. New York: AMS Press, 1975.

Thalbitzer, William (1914–41) 'The Ammassalik Eskimo: contribution to the ethnology of the East Greenland natives', *Meddelelser om Gronland*, vols 39–40, 53. Copenhagen.

Turner, Lucien M. (1894) 'Ethnology of the Ungava District, Hudson Bay Territory', *Eleventh Annual Report of the Bureau of American Ethnology, Smithsonian Institution*, Washington, DC: Government Printing Office, pp. 159–350; Quebec: Comeditex Presses, 1979.

Van Maanen, John (1988) *Tales of the Field: On Writing Ethnography*, Chicago and London: University of Chicago Press.

Vdovin, Innokentii S. (1965) *Ocherki istorii i etnografii chukchei*, Moscow and Leningrad: Nauka.

Vinnikov, I. N. (1935) 'Bibliografiia etnograficheskikh i lingvisticheskikh rabot V. G. Bogoraza', *Sovetskaia etnografiia*, 4–5: 235–41.

Chapter 4

The concept of culture between modernity and postmodernity

Carla Pasquinelli

THE WEAKEST LINK

Culture seems to have become a commonplace word serving to recycle terms which have lost their communicative effectiveness. Expressions such as 'rock culture' or 'drug culture' – to cite only some of the most common – are now part of our everyday language. The term culture serves to create a halo of allusiveness, projecting the words beyond their literal meaning into a broader semantic context.

Though the popularity of a scientific category is a sure sign of its success, its final outcome seems in this case largely negative. Culture is becoming a dangerously unfocused term, increasingly lacking in scientific credentials, and this fact has brought many anthropologists to distance themselves from it. Indeed, the popularity of the concept outside anthropology is strikingly in contrast with its eccentric position within the discipline, where culture seems in the process of becoming a marginal category, destined perhaps to an imminent demise. Even without taking Gellner's extreme position, for whom culture is 'a sort of proto-concept' that anthropologists could very well do without, few scholars feel comfortable defending this category, at least openly.

There is nothing very surprising in this, after all. The vulgarisation of a category is always a risky operation, where that which is gained in currency is lost in rigour, as the increased semantic burden inevitably augments the term's ambiguity. I do not think, however, that the popularity of the term alone can explain the diffidence anthropologists display towards it, though it may have been a compounding factor. In the same way, I disagree with those who maintain that there is nothing new in this crisis inasmuch as 'the idea of culture has been in crisis from the moment it began to take distinct shape' (Herbert 1991: 17). While the latter statement may be true, it does not help us very much to

understand the specific nature of the current crisis. In fact, looking back
to the past for an explanation could even put us on a false track, since,
besides hindering our understanding of the new factors at play, it would
run the risk of reducing this crisis to an endemic phenomenon, the late
manifestation of original aporias. Indeed, in my view, the most
important and novel factor is that the present crisis does not originate
from within the concept of culture. Rather it is an imported crisis, being
a consequence of the violent impact of postmodern criticism on
anthropological paradigms. Indeed, postmodern criticism seems to have
singled out the concept of culture as the weakest link of the discipline,
and the consequences for this category have been devastating. Thus, the
concept of culture runs the risk of disappearing under the cross-fire of
rival paradigms, modernism and postmodernism, based on different
truth criteria, which have found precisely in the concept of culture their
fiercest battleground.

THINKING ALL FORMS OF OTHERNESS

The concept of culture is in this uncomfortable position at the centre of
the clash between modern and postmodern because it is firmly rooted in
modernity. It is well known that the concept of culture arose within
evolutionist theory. However, if we wish to go further and place it in a
broader context, we must acknowledge that it is a product of modernity
at least as much as anthropology itself.

As for other social sciences, the bases of cultural anthropology are to
be found in the development in scientific knowledge that characterised
modernity. Yet, compared to other social sciences anthropology has a
very special relationship to modernity, since, while being a product of
modernity, it is also one of its foundations, in the sense that
anthropology is essential to modernity's self-representation. The
concept of modern cannot be defined without referring to that which
is not modern. In other words, it needs an external reference point in
order to define itself by difference.

Anthropology provides this reference point by assuming as its object
of inquiry what could be loosely termed pre-modern societies. The
modern, however, does not proceed from here as one would perhaps
expect, that is, defining itself in relation to pre-modern societies;
instead, it defines the latter in relation to itself. In other words, it
'reclassifies in relation to itself ages and civilizations distant in time and
space, ordering them and denominating them from its own centrality –
e.g.: the primitive, the Middle Ages, underdeveloped countries, etc.'

(Pasquinelli 1985: 13). Thus modernity reaffirms its centrality, subordinating and refunctionalising others to it. Yet, modernity cannot do without these others, since it depends on them for its own self-representation, albeit (herein lies its ideological character) establishing with them an asymmetrical relationship and assuming the dominant position.

The concept of culture plays a fundamental, indeed, a founding role in this process. Culture is the category that enables one to conceive all forms of otherness in relation to which the modern defines itself by difference. It becomes the container of everything that is not modern, in two ways: it contains the past, what is called tradition, and it contains that vast part of the present that occurs outside the boundaries of western civilisation, namely, to use an increasingly rare expression, primitive societies.

Thus, anthropology is the offspring of modernity, yet, paradoxically, it accepts and acknowledges all that negates it. More precisely, anthropology is the instrument created by modernity to represent its own negation.

TYLOR

The concept of culture is located inside modernity, not only for the reasons stated above, but particularly because it is epistemologically grounded within modernity.

The idea of reason and the idea of progress are the two central features of modernity. Modernity is dominated by the idea of a strong reason providing totalising interpretations of the world (Rossi 1989: 39) and emancipating humanity through a history that is endowed with meaning. This history is characterised by a linear time, which develops in a progressive, ceaseless fashion toward a future that is constantly to be superseded. Modernity is, as Gianni Vattimo says, 'the era of superseding, of novelty that grows old and is substituted by a newer novelty' (Vattimo 1985: 11).

If we take into account the first, Tylor's formulation of the concept of culture (1871), it will easily be shown that these two intertwined notions constitute the theoretical framework for Tylor's interpretation of culture: 'Culture or civilization, taken in its ethnographic sense is that complex whole which includes knowledge, belief, art, morals, law, custom, and any other capabilities and habits acquired by man as a member of society' (Tylor 1951: 3). What gives this definition ethnographic significance is the idea that this array of disparate elements of social life makes up a 'complex whole', a totality, and that all the elements of this whole are dependent on one another. Culture as such is not society's beliefs, customs, moral values, and so forth, added together: it is the wholeness that their co-existence somehow creates or makes manifest.

This position reveals a holistic vision that is remarkably in contrast with dominating trends in Anglo-Saxon social sciences of the period, but can be explained by taking into account the strong influence of German thought on Tylor. As Joan Leopold has proved in an interesting study published a few years ago, 'the "complex whole" was in Germany a common idea of the early 19th century' (Leopold 1980: 105). In particular, Tylor was familiar with it via Gustav Klemm with whom he had a close relationship which strongly influenced his theoretical positions. Indeed, Tylor's concept of culture itself was taken from Klemm who, as Kluckhohn and Kroeber remind us, had been the first to use it in place of civilisation (Kluckhohn and Kroeber 1963: 49).

Klemm's influence was decisive for the future of the discipline which retained the holistic orientation characteristic of Tylor's notion of culture, even if, as Joan Leopold observes, 'Tylor', unlike Klemm, 'did not say that this "complex whole" was "organic" as Klemm and others might have. For Tylor, parts could be separated, though not completely, for study' (Leopold 1989: 105). Along with the idea of totality, another distinctive trait of modernity appears in Tylor's definition: the idea of progress, which enables him to create the majestic scenario of cultural evolution, which progresses from simple to more complex stages, according to an evolutionary and progressive conception of time that, as we noted above, is typical of modernity.

Thus, the concept of culture is born with two godparents, the idea of organic totality and the idea of a linear, progressive time, providing it with the characteristics tokens of modernity. From modernity, the concept of culture inherits its evolutionary optimism and the ambition to control the most remote recesses of reality.

DEMOCRACY AND HIERARCHY

There is a third reason why the concept of culture may be considered a product of modernity: its egalitarian, democratic character. Thanks to this, the attribute of culture could be assigned to that vast area of humanity that western civilisation had always considered closer to nature. Instead of the chaotic ensemble of strange, incomprehensible customs that for centuries had filled with diffident wonder travellers' notebooks and the Western world at large, the concept of culture provides us with a 'complex whole' wherein those customs attain order and meaning. The concept of culture makes the primitive thinkable, endows it with form, makes its representation possible. Through it, primitive populations are brought within the same order of reality to which we westerners belong. We all become part of the same history, the same cultural evolution.

Yet, it is precisely in this genealogical acknowledgement, in itself undoubtably an important step toward a more tolerant attitude, that the ethnocentrism of the concept of culture lies hidden. We are like them and they are like us, but between us and them lies time, that linear time that sets us at the top and them at the bottom of cultural evolution. If culture has brought us closer, the idea of progress re-creates an insurmountable distance between us, in the form of a rigid hierarchy.

Thus, Tylor's notion of culture is not free from a measure of ethnocentrism, since the irradiating origin of the perspective from which the primitive is viewed remains the Western world. This ethnocentrism is based on a double negation: the negation of history and negation of otherness. History as an indistinct multiplicity of unique events is negated and reduced to a single vector moving in a uniform, progressive fashion from simple to complex. Otherness is also negated, in so far as differences are arranged only on a vertical axis, appearing as mere quantitative variations in cultural evolution, which becomes, thus, hierarchically ordained.

AN ETHNOCENTRIC WHOLE

With Boas, the concept of culture meets history and differences become prominent. Culture disappears and is replaced by a plurality of cultures, while history breaks on to the scene, dissolving Tylor's rigid evolutionary scheme into a variety of potential paths. With Boas, the original sin of ethnocentrism seems to be cleansed and cultural relativism takes the spotlight.

I do not intend to address the complex ethical and epistemological problems created by the theory of cultural relativism. I only wish to stress how Boas has enriched the concept of culture with a new attribute: its relational character. Cultures now make up an articulated scenario where the single protagonist is replaced by a plurality of subjects, who have to deal with a complex cohabitation. Independently from the difficult issue of communication arising from the existence of a plurality of cultures – cultural relativism being one of the possible ways of addressing it – this plurality highlights the relational character of culture. Since culture has been replaced by a plurality of cultures, each culture needs the existence of the others for its recognition and self-definition. This relativism, however, tends to undermine the paradigms of modernity, within which, as we have seen, the concept of culture is inscribed. As Roy Wagner has pointed out: 'The classical rationalistic pretence of absolute objectivity must be given up in favor of a relative objectivity based on the characteristics of one's own culture' (1975: 2). Hence, it is not surprising that so much attention has been paid by postmodern criticism to cultural relativism and that Geertz sees Boas as his immediate predecessor, questions I will examine more extensively further on.

Thus, beginning with Boas, the concept of culture loses its ethnocentric stigma. Yet, it does not free itself completely from ethnocentrism. Up to here, ethnocentrism seemed an accessory, something added from without, the product of a notion of progress setting the Western world at the top and primitive populations at the bottom of cultural evolution. In fact, ethnocentrism is far more intrinsic to the concept of culture, indeed, it is a fundamental element of its structure.

Although much of the theoretical framework within which the concept of culture arises changes with Boas, something is retained, something abounding in the many and often contradictory definitions of culture that mark the history of anthropology, as can be easily verified by examining the definitions of culture collected in the anthology edited by Kluckhohn and Kroeber (1963). It is the idea of 'complex whole', although Boas prefers the word 'totality' or 'structure'. Now, it is precisely this idea of totality or 'complex whole', this 'myth of cultural integration' as Margaret S. Archer has defined it (1983), that raises the suspicion of ethnocentrism. If culture is our essential tool for constructing the other, and if culture is a product of modernity, then this other must necessarily pattern itself according to the paradigms of modernity. In other words, to be acknowledged as such, every culture must present itself as a 'complex whole', thus conforming to the model produced by modernity. In this way, every culture becomes the projection of the strong paradigms of the modern idea of reason.

The suspicion of ethnocentrism becomes certainty with Roy Wagner, albeit for different reasons. For Wagner too, the anthropological concept of culture is a western projection; however, this does not derive from its relationship with the nucleus of the modern idea of reason, as much as, more simply, from its being an extension of the élitist meaning of the term culture. 'As long as the anthropological concept remains even partially dependent upon the opera house sense of the term our studies of other people and particularly of tribal societies will be skewed in the direction of our own self image' (1975: 30). In both cases, however, a perverse mechanism is at play, which tends to superimpose our image on others. In this way, culture becomes the very metaphor of order, our order, and any description of others becomes a way to speak of ourselves.

THE MATERIAL PHASE

The notion of 'complex whole' remains a constant feature in the various interpretations of culture. What varies, though, is the content of the concept, the elements that are considered as falling under the heading of culture. In fact, it is the dominance of one particular element over the others that gives interpretations their distinctive character.

Three important cultural features have characterised three different phases in the history of anthropology: customs, patterns and meanings. These in turn correspond to three different methodological paradigms: explanation, understanding, interpretation.

Tylor's definition, as everybody knows, is the broadest possible, including 'any capabilities and habits acquired by man as a member of society' (Tylor 1871: vol. 1). Custom, however, emerges as the dominant element in his definition, and this inclusion must have seemed outrageous at the time, notwithstanding the fact that, in acknowledging the importance of custom, Tylor was only following in the footsteps of Herodotus and Montaigne. In fact, one gets the impression that Tylor was deliberately emphasising one of the aspects that had been most excluded from the realm of culture, in its élitist sense. While knowledge, beliefs, art, morals, law, have always been considered part of culture, custom had always represented their antithesis. While art and morals are universals, customs are material and specific, the local behavioural patterns according to which people organise their lives. Making custom a structural element of the new concept of culture, beside highlighting its importance, emphasised the epistemological break that the new concept of culture creates within the established paradigms of western thought.

The centrality of custom is typical of what we may define as the *material phase* of the concept of culture. From a methodological perspective this phase is based, as we already noted, on the explanation paradigm. In this first phase, anthropology follows in the wake of other social sciences, which adopted the method of natural sciences, based on the identification of uniformities, the formulation of laws, and the absolute belief in the objective character of the investigated phenomena. Within this paradigm, custom plays a central role in guaranteeing the objective nature that Durkheim attributes to social facts, or, more precisely, to our way of apprehending them.

This phase, perhaps for its novel and subversive character, has been more influential than any other outside the boundaries of anthropology, and has decisively enhanced the prestige of the discipline.

KINSHIPS AND DEBTS

Anthropology has often been at the centre of a peculiar asymmetrical exchange with neighbouring disciplines, particularly history, sociology and philosophy. One could speak of an influence of anthropology, if the appropriation of anthropological methods and concepts by other disciplines were not carried out in a very furtive fashion and with a depressing dearth of due thanks. What I am concerned with, however, is stressing that the go-between in this transaction is, in most cases, Tylor's notion of culture. As far as philosophy is concerned, I am referring particularly to the later Wittgenstein. As the Italian anthropologist Francesco Remotti has accurately shown (1990), Wittgenstein, in his *Philosophical Investigations*, breaks with the tradition of Cartesian rationalism, acknowledging the role played by culture, and especially custom, in the very structure of reason. Customs – Wittgenstein prefers the expression 'forms of life' – tend to deprive Descartes' *cogito* of its absolute hold over reason, introducing the dimension of 'we'. Customs, 'forms of life', represent the revenge of the particular against the idea of a universal and natural reason. Certainly, the merit and responsibility of what is no doubt an epistemological revolution cannot be ascribed solely to anthropology. But it may be that, without the anthropological concept of culture, this revolution would not have been even thinkable. Even Herder, who in some ways anticipates Tylor – it is well known that Herder went close to formulating the anthropological concept of culture – lacks a category that would enable him to strongly formalise the dominant role of custom over reason.

Another discipline that owes much to the anthropological concept of culture is history. With the group centred around *Annales* the concept of culture – under the disguise of the category of *mentalité* – entered the discipline of history radically altering its methods and approaches. The category of *mentalité* – the English term, mentality, is not an adequate translation since, as Le Goff observes (Le Goff and Nora 1974), it has a much more cognitive, intellectual connotation – was more circumscribed than Tylor's notion of culture and in some ways more elusive, less definable. *Mentalité* is described as a passive substrate that determines our whole way of being. It is the style of a period, a society's connective tissue, the historical sedimentation of collective thoughts and actions, manifesting itself in people's gestures, behaviours, habits. It implies the idea of an unconscious force to which collective automatisms must be ascribed, suggesting therefore a certain inertia due, perhaps, to the influence of Lév-Bruhl and structuralism.

These are only two examples, yet I think they are quite striking and serve sufficiently to prove the influence of Tylor's concept of culture outside the boundaries of anthropology. At any rate, the historians of *mentalité* are the first to acknowledge their debt towards anthropological studies, although they are reluctant to admit a direct and immediate descendance. In this, they are quite right, since this influence was gradually exerted over a long period of time, the time necessary for any subversive notion to become part of what Gramsci defines as 'common sense'. However, Tylor's concept of culture, paradoxically, began to exert its influence outside anthropology precisely when it was no longer dominant within the discipline.

This influence seems destined to extend itself in the future, and has recently manifested itself in political thought. I am referring to the important role played by the neo-communitarians' position in the American debate, whose criticism of both individualists and universalists is based on a notion of community that seems closer to Tylor than to Tönnies. For neo-communitarians the notion of good is simply the manifestation in terms of values of the culture of a particular social group. This third example, to which many others could be added, confirms the tendency of the concept of culture to get rid of its disciplinary boundaries and become part of contemporary discourse.

THE ABSTRACT PHASE

In the 1930s, anthropologists' attention began shifting from customs to 'behaviour patterns'. This was not an easy transition, as witnessed by the lively discussion that developed during those years and continued, with various ups and downs, until the 1950s, finally resulting in a narrowing of the concept of culture. It no longer included 'any capabilities and habits acquired by man as a member of society'. Instead, it was restricted to value systems and normative models that regulate the behaviour of the members of a given social group. In spite of this drastic limitation, the notion of culture as a 'complex whole' was retained. In fact, it became even more essential since it guaranteed the coherence necessary to any normative system. In this second phase, which could be defined as the *abstract phase* of culture, due to a marked shift of interest towards collective representations, a process of abstraction began, which transformed the notion of culture into that of a conceptual system existing independently from any social practice. To define culture in terms of patterns of behaviour instead of social habits, to conceive it as a value system, means, as Kluckhohn and Kroeber (1963) have noted, attributing to it an abstract character.

This restricted interpretation of the concept of culture had important effects at a methodological level. Once the material character of culture is questioned, so is the utility of the naturalistic paradigm. The notion that culture is a set of shared models which, more or less consciously, shapes the behaviour and actions of people, requires a more adequate paradigm, closer to that of understanding sociology. But the merit of making this fact explicit cannot be ascribed to anthropologists, whose position remains rather ambiguous. While on the one hand they absorbed through Boas the neo-Kantian distinction between natural sciences (*Naturwissenschaften*) and 'cultural' or 'human' sciences (*Geisteswissenschaften*), between nomothetic and idiographic approaches, on the other they did not appear interested in drawing out the ultimate consequences. Instead, they either avoided the problem or, like Kroeber, they remained obstinately committed to the naturalistic method. Instead, it was the sociologists, specifically Parsons, who, having adopted the concept of culture, were responsible for connecting it to the understanding method.

In this second phase – the abstract phase – the concept of culture exercised a noticeable influence on other disciplines, particularly sociology and psychology, which used it to explore, from opposite perspectives, the delicate and magmatic ties between society and individuals. The concept of culture as a set of values and models shared by a given social group is, for these disciplines, the category that enables them to define a level of social reality which, while closely interrelated with the social system as well as intrapsychic ones, remains distinct from them in social consciousness.

To outline all the effects produced by the adoption of this concept of culture is practically impossible since it would entail recounting the last fifty years of the history of these two disciplines. For both of them the concept of culture is not an occasional or sporadic presence. Instead it has become, in different ways, an essential part of their theoretical systems. This influence is very different from the one anthropology has exercised over other disciplines, such as philosophy and history, to which we have referred above; not only on account of the continuative character of the relationship and the effect it had on theoretical paradigms, but also for its non-univocal character, given the complex exchange which develops between the respective areas of competence. Anthropological speculation on the concept of culture has been continually stimulated by feedback from sociology and psychology. The most emblematic example of this interdisciplinary interaction is surely that of Parsons. His use of the concept of culture is never passive. Parsons takes up the concept of culture as value models shaping social action in order to explain the relationship between social system and personality, but he develops the concept in ways which exerted an important influence on anthropology. This last fact has been recently highlighted in an article by Adam Kuper, who sees Parsons as the archetype of the Geertzian interpretation of culture as a system of symbols (Kuper 1994: 540).

The relationship between anthropology and psychology, too, is not lacking in reciprocal influences. To trace these, one must necessarily refer, above all, to the culture and personality school, which was the outcome of a complex network of debts and credits between the two disciplines.

This joint reflection on the same theme ended up creating through the years a form of contiguity, confronting anthropologists with the need to differentiate themselves from sociologists in their use of a rather similar concept of culture. This need was often addressed through endless reformulations of the concept of culture, to which the charge of magically solving the problems of disciplinary identity has been delegated. This trend towards new definitions of the concept – Kluckhohn and Kroeber (1963) have counted more than 250 – was the main limit to the debate on culture to which we referred above, since all too often the debate on the proper definition took the place of more serious reflection. While this has served to draw attention to a concept which had often been taken for granted in the past, its final outcome has been the increasing vagueness of the term, due perhaps to its overuse. Thus, at the height of its prestige outside the discipline, the concept of culture ceased to be of interest to anthropologists and practically disappeared from the anthropological scene. For good, we might add, since it has never again been a crucial subject of reflection and discussion. In other words, it seems to have exhausted its potentialities.

THE SYMBOLIC PHASE

In this general climate of indifference, the concept of culture enters its third phase, which I would call the *symbolic phase*. Again its content changes. Culture becomes a 'web of significance', or, more precisely, 'culture consists of socially established structures of meaning' (Geertz 1983: 50). Geertz's definition, while being so well known as to make its detailed description superfluous, has not, in my opinion, been paid enough attention. Probably because while offering it an important role in his interpretative anthropology, Geertz ends up by assigning it a marginal one in his writings. Culture for Geertz, as he himself states, is essentially a semiotic concept. Culture is seen as a text, a text written by the natives, which the anthropologist must interpret. In so doing, he must take the natives' interpretation into account. Therefore, his knowledge consists of interpretations of interpretations. Culture, thus, becomes a system of signs socially constructed at the moment of their interpretation. According to Geertz, to interpret is to impose an order. But this order is a local one, and the anthropologist's knowledge is a local knowledge, too. Hence, Geertz's position is relativistic, although his relativism is somewhat peculiar, inasmuch as it does not exclude the possibility of understanding the other. Indeed, Geertz seems almost to take this possibility for granted, when, with an unexpected retreat into common sense, he says that 'accounts of other people's subjectivities can be built up without recourse to pretensions to more-than-normal capacities for ego effacement and fellow feeling' (Geertz 1983: 70). Geertz is a true relativist, instead, in his irresistible, fatal attraction toward what is particular. Culture is always factual, specific and unique. Its diversity must therefore be guarded from any attempt to find universals. Thus, Geertz, too, elaborates 'a narrowed, specialized concept of culture' for he considers it 'theoretically more powerful' (1973: 40).

In asserting his own definition of culture, Geertz feels the need to keep aloof from all other definitions, including Tylor's, whom he, too, criticises for his notion of 'complex whole'. While not denying its 'originative power', Geertz states that it 'seems to have reached the point where it obscures a good deal more than it reveals' (1973: 4).

Yet, in actual practice, Geertz retains much more of past interpretations of the concept of culture, pertaining both to the material and to the abstract phase, than he is willing to admit. Without concerning himself too much with the contradictions he sometimes falls into, Geertz proves himself to be a wise administrator of the entire anthropological heritage, on which he draws whenever it is convenient.

Thus, as has often been pointed out by his most severe critics, but also by others closer to him, he often says something and its opposite. On the one hand, he defines culture as a system of meanings; on the other hand, he is not above resorting to other definitions, speaking of customs, behaviour patterns, or value systems. In other words, he uses as resources precisely those interpretations he has rejected a few pages earlier. Thus, while on the one hand, culture is considered to be the anthropologist's construction, on the other, it appears to exist independently as an objective, or even natural, datum, almost an intrinsic property of things. This ambivalence is evident, for example, in his distinction between '(Moroccan) culture as a natural fact and (Moroccan) culture as a theoretical entity' (Geertz 1973: 15), which suggests the existence of an objective *quid* that cannot be reduced to the anthropologist's or the native's interpretation.

The ambivalence becomes even more pronounced in the distinction made by Geertz between 'experience-near concepts', and 'experience-distant concepts', in order to indicate two different interpretative approaches, the first pertaining to the natives, and the second to the anthropologist. With this distinction, closely resembling the one between etic and emic made in cognitive anthropology, Geertz recovers the idea of an interpretative paradigm that is not only independent from local native interpretations but, in fact, superimposed upon them. Thus, Geertz reintroduces a variety of generalisation that is hardly consistent with his theory of local knowledge. Indeed, even Geertz admits that his relativism does not exclude the possibility of generalisations, so long as 'experience-distant' concepts are placed in 'illuminating connection' with concepts which for another people are 'experience-near' (Geertz 1983: 58). It would be, therefore, difficult to disagree with those that say that interpretative anthropology risks replacing generalisations on behaviour with generalisations on meaning.

Finally, while severely critical of Tylor's notion of 'complex whole', Geertz himself ends up by resorting to it. When talking of thick description, referring to the operation performed by the ethnologist in discovering and reconstructing levels of meaning that are not explicit to the actor's perspectives, in practice, he reintroduces and uses the notion of totality. His 'thick description' is nothing but an updated version of the hermeneutic circle that Geertz defines in the following way: 'hopping back and forth the whole conceived through the parts that actualize it and the parts conceived through the whole that motivates them' (1983: 69). It is not clear whether this is meant to be an interpretative procedure or an intrinsic characteristic of objects.

The impression one gets is that ambivalence is an integral part of Geertz's thought. I do not think, however, that it is a question of personal uncertainties. Rather I feel that he is simply evidencing a general crisis of our discipline, characterised by a conflict between opposite paradigms. Geertz's position is liminal since it is located at the boundary between postmodern and modern, between a local knowledge dispersed among a plurality of unrelated fragments and the nostalgia for strong paradigms.

Geertz's notion of culture seems to be the product of the difficult quest for a middle point. The concept of culture is entrusted with the mission of retaining some kind of unitary meaning within the dispersed plurality of local knowledges to which anthropology seems condemned by the current dominance of the interpretative paradigm.

THE NARRATING I

With James Clifford this ambiguity is finally resolved in favour of one of its two aspects (Clifford and Marcus 1986: 242). It is the triumph of postmodernism in anthropology. With a curious time lag, as Paul Rabinow has, somewhat sarcastically, noted, anthropologists are 'now discovering and being moved to new creation by the infusion of ideas from deconstructionist literary criticism now that it has lost its cultural energy in literature departments' (1986: 242).

Whether *parvenu* or Cinderella, anthropology, an eleventh-hour arrival to the tolerant postmodern world, seems to have finally found the solution to its problems. Tylor's notion of 'complex whole' has been definitely set aside along with the concept of culture. They are no longer needed. The only true hero is the anthropologist's narrating I, which replaces the object to be described. At first glance, James Clifford's work seems to follow naturally in the wake of Geertz's interpretative turn. However, as Paul Rabinow, again, notes, there is a major difference:

> Geertz . . . is still directing his efforts to reinvent an anthropological science with the help of textual mediations. The core activity is still social description of the other, however modified by new concep-tions of discourse, author, or text. The other for Clifford is the anthropological representation of the other.
>
> (1986: 242)

With Clifford, anthropology retreats from the world into the text. The text is the only thing that counts, and culture is reduced to fiction or, to use one of Clifford's favourite oxymorons, a 'true fiction'. 'Culture is not an object to be described, neither is it a unified corpus of symbols and meanings that can be definitively interpreted' (Clifford and Marcus 1986: 19). 'Culture and our views of 'it' are produced historically' (1986: 18). 'Cultural is contested, temporal, and emergent' (1986: 19). While he continues to refer to the concept of culture, it is obvious that the term has acquired a quite different meaning, or, as Talal Asad writes, 'this notion of culture . . . was transformed into the notion of a *text* – that is, into something resembling an inscribed discourse' (1986: 141). With this we are fully in the postmodern scenario. Even disciplinary boundaries are blurred, and a spurious, unstable, partial knowledge takes over.

It is difficult to decide how much of this is the product of an internal crisis of anthropology that has been in the making for a long time, and how much of it is the product of a long-overdue show-down between modern and postmodern within the discipline. In fact, the two things seem to coincide, which is not surprising, given that, as we have seen, the concept of culture is intimately connected to modernity, and cannot thus escape being affected by the crisis of the latter's paradigms.

If, as Lyotard says, postmodernism marks the end of meta-narratives, then this end of meta-narratives cannot help involving a concept like culture. Not only because the concept of culture has its roots in modernity, but especially because it has been the instrument of master narratives, which have enabled modernity to represent the other. Anthropology is a narrative knowledge, which has found in the concept of culture its method and legitimisation. In particular, the organic metaphor of the 'complex whole' has made it possible to perceive communities as perfectly integrated and unified totalities. The ethnographer is faced with the problem of translating the multiplicity of experience into a coherent whole and, as Robert Thornton notes, this is possible only if one is able to imagine the wholes and 'convey this imagination of wholeness to his reader' (1992: 15), since 'social wholes can not be directly experienced by a single human observer' (1992: 18). The concept of culture is the artifice that has enabled imagination to perceive coherent wholes. The artifice has been made more successful by the use of that 'free indirect style', that hides or neutralises the observer's gaze, transforming her or him into a passive spectator of a pre-defined scenario.

Clifford has the merit of having uncovered this narrative artifice. He was set on the right track by Michel de Certeau's anticipatory writings, which concentrated, more than on the rhetorical techniques through which the anthropological text stages the other, on what is lost of native culture when it is translated in our categories (de Certeau 1988: 202). For Clifford, however, the scandal does not lie in what is lost as much as in what is gained. What often passes for the natives' point of view is really the anthropologist's, who, in translating from one language to the other – and, as Talal Asad reminds us, language stands for 'modes of thought' – makes the described culture coincide with the text's production, subjecting it to 'relations of "weak" and "strong" languages that govern the international flow of knowledge' (Clifford and Marcus 1986: 22).

Having uncovered the artifice, Clifford seems to fall in love with it, since, with a curious form of symbolic inversion, he transforms into a virtue what he had previously criticised as a serious defect, turning it into a general rule, legitimising it and reducing anthropological knowledge to a text. The other disappears, and its place is triumphantly taken by the anthropologist's narrating I. Thus, the most extreme form of relativism, which postmodernity legitimises and valorises, takes on an ethnocentric cast. The text, which has gradually replaced the object, reflects our own image. The other leaves its place to the projection of the omnipotent 'we'.

Anthropology appears to be incapable of freeing itself from its godparent ethnocentrism. Paradoxically, extreme relativism ends up by engendering an even more radical ethnocentrism than the one it sought to attack. From this perspective, the idea of a dialogical anthropology proposed by Clifford, where the text is no longer a product of the anthropologist but arises from the encounter between observer and observed, is unconvincing, since it is completely at odds with his relativism. That is, unless one is to apply this method solely to complex societies, which are realistically the only case where the anthropologist can be at once the observer and the observed.

THE CRISIS OF THE CRISIS

The crisis of anthropological paradigms must, therefore, be inscribed within the general crisis of modernity and considered as an episode in the clash between modern and postmodern: a long-standing conflict between two alternative paradigms, understanding and interpretive, which has found in anthropology its last battleground and for this reason has been especially vicious and devastating.

Compared to the aporias that confronted social sciences at the beginning of the century, bringing about the decline of the naturalistic paradigm, the ones facing anthropologists now are diametrically

opposite. While previously the problem that prompted the adoption of
the understanding paradigm was the unsettling discovery that the object
of inquiry in social sciences coincided with the inquiring subject,
nowadays the problem is the complete split between the two. The dis-
homogeneity between observer and observed exposes the limitations of
the understanding paradigm, and explains the adoption of the
interpretive paradigm, which delegates to the responsibility of the
observer the very existence of the observed.

While the current difficulties of anthropology should be set within
this broader scenario, yet one should not underrate the intrinsic reasons
for this crisis, whose origin, as we have seen, dates further back. It
would be more correct to state, perhaps, that the clash between modern
and postmodern has entered anthropology thanks to the vacuum left by
the crisis of the concept of culture.

It is not the first time that the concept of culture is questioned, but it
is the first time that anthropology seems to be able or willing to do
without it. To cite a well-known expression of the American ecology
movement, once anthropologists, were people who 'thought globally
and acted locally'. Nowadays they are restricted to thinking and acting
locally. The end of meta-narratives seems to have decreed our
confinement to a local knowledge, that finds in itself its own
interpretive categories, and anthropology appears to have done away
with the concept of culture for good.

Yet, this is far less true than some would have us believe. In
fieldwork, the concept of culture continues to be a useful tool,
imparting order and meaning to empirical materials. And anthropological discourse is still characterised by the ill-famed 'free indirect
style', James Clifford's work being no exception. As Paul Rabinow has
noted, 'Clifford talks a great deal about the ineluctability of dialogue
(thereby establishing his authority as an "open" one), but his texts are
not themselves dialogic' (1986: 244).

Are we faced, then, with a split between empirical research and
theoretical reflection? Is culture doomed to become a mere archaism, a
category used only in certain peripheral and backward areas of the
discipline? According to Gellner (1985), this is what is happening.
Culture, as we have seen, is considered a sort of 'proto-concept', rather
inadequate and imprecise. Something we can do without.

Yet, the idea of a discipline that gets rid of its founding categories is
rather implausible. In general, it is hard to conceive of a science that
can do without a system of categories that enables it to avoid being
trapped in local knowledges. Furthermore, local knowledge in itself,

based exclusively on the natives' interpretations, is ungraspable to anybody, including Geertz himself, who, as we have seen, is finally forced to resort to more general concepts.

THE THIRD PATH

I am under the impression that the deconstructionist hurricane has left us with a conspicuous nostalgia for strong paradigms. While thanks to deconstructionism our categories have lost their innocence and previously taken-for-granted concepts and discursive styles have been questioned, deconstructionism itself has proved incapable of drawing the line at the point where a discipline runs the risk of being destroyed by the deconstruction of its own paradigms.

As far as the concept of culture is concerned, drawing this line is no easy task. Certainly, we cannot ignore the fact that the concept of culture itself is a local knowledge. It is a paradigm arising out of our own local knowledge, out of our 'forms of life', yet aspiring to a universal status. And these universal aspirations themselves are part of our local knowledge. Let us try to break this vicious circle somehow. For example, we may consider the fact that while the concept of culture is at its historical nadir, this does not hold true for the adjective 'cultural'. In its adjectival form, the concept of culture is reappearing with the support of other categories. I am thinking especially of the category of identity. The expression 'cultural identity' is increasingly used in place of 'culture'.

It is difficult to draw univocal inferences from this linguistic shift. It could indicate either a tendency to get rid of the concept of culture, or to reintroduce it in a way that somehow bypasses its limitations, transferring to the category of identity the need for totality and coherence that the concept of culture no longer can legitimately satisfy. Certainly, it is a symptom of the need for strong paradigms, for categories that can serve to reduce complexity, to select among the unrelated multiplicity that local knowledge seems unable to control. In itself, the concept of culture, thanks to the notion of 'complex whole', is a formidable reducer of complexity that enables one to select among the surplus of meanings and possibilities that any object of research offers. What appears obsolete is its organic structure, the idea of a 'complex whole' in which all elements are held together by a unifying principle.

But what remains of the concept of culture, once liberated, if this is possible, from the idea of 'complex whole'? Furthermore, is it enough to eliminate the idea of 'complex whole' to get rid of ethnocentrism altogether? And should we really get rid of ethnocentrism? We have learned by now that besides being impossible for anybody to escape her or his 'forms of life', it is probably also undesirable. It is only by accepting the partiality of their point of view that anthropologists can trust their categories, keeping control over the ethnocentrism which, while inevitably conditioning their research, guarantees their rooted-ness in their 'form of life'. This was understood long ago by Ernesto De Martino, who referred to 'critical ethnocentrism', an expression that was not very successful due to its polemical connotations, but which perhaps should be taken up again. According to De Martino, the encounter with the other can only be experienced from our specific ethnocentric perspective, but at the same time it offers us a chance to distance ourselves and question our culture. 'Critical ethnocentrism' takes this chance.

As Pietro Clemente has observed, there are significant similarities between De Martino's 'critical ethnocentrism' and Geertz's interpretive paradigm (Clemente 1991: 62). While Geertz's and De Martino's positions arise from different contexts and historical periods, they are both the product of the effort to find a 'third path' beyond relativism and ethnocentrism, and both insist on the relational character of the ethnographic encounter. For both, it is impossible to experience the other without experiencing oneself at the same time, and only this simultaneity guarantees a reciprocal intelligibility. But while for Geertz and, to some extent, for dialogic anthropology, the 'broading of self-awareness' is prevalently designed to understand the other's 'form of life', De Martino's attention is focused exclusively on the Western world. Both tend to search for a meaning that makes the other and oneself intelligible, but De Martino is usually interested in the encounter with the *ethnos* only in so far as it allows the opportunity, as De Martino states (echoing a famous passage by Lévi-Strauss), to 'question the system in which one was born and raised' (1980: 140). This choice appears to him the only possibility of 'freeing oneself from the so-called Western ethnocentrisms' (1980: 135).

Acceptance of our categories, beginning with culture, in all the partiality characteristic of our 'form of life,' remains, after so many years, a road that must yet be travelled and one of the few ones left.

Translated by Gabriele Poole

72   Carla Pasquinelli

REFERENCES

Abbagnano, N. (1962) 'Il relativismo culturale', *Quaderni di sociologia*, 2: 5–22.
Archer, M.S. (1988) *Culture and Agency: The Place of Culture in Social Theory*, Cambridge, Mass.: Cambridge University Press.
Asad, T. (1986) 'The concept of cultural translation', in J. Clifford and G. Marcus (eds), *Writing Culture: The Poetics and Politics of Ethnography*, Berkeley and Los Angeles: University of California Press, pp. 141–64.
Boas, F. (1938) *The Mind of Primitive Man*, New York: Macmillan.
Certeau, M. de (1988) *The Writing of History*, New York: Columbia University Press.
Clemente, P. (1991) 'Oltre Geertz: scrittura e documentazione demologica', *L'Uomo* IV, NS, 1: 57–96.
Clifford, J. (1988) *The Predicament of Culture: Twentieth-Century Ethnography, Literature and Art*, Cambridge: Harvard University Press.
Clifford, J. and Marcus, G. (eds) (1986) *Writing Culture: The Poetics and Politics of Ethnography*, Berkeley and Los Angeles: University of California Press.
De Martino, E. (1980) *Furore Simbolo Valore*, Milan: Feltrinelli.
Dei, F. and Simonicca, A. (eds) (1990) *Ragione e forme di vita: Razionalismo e relativismo in antropologia*, Milan: Franco Angeli.
Fabietti, U. (1991) 'Relativismo, oggettivismo, ragione antropologica', *L'Uomo* IV, NS, 1: 21–39.
Geertz, C. (1973) *The Interpretation of Cultures*, New York: Basic Books.
—— (1979) *Meaning and Order in Moroccan Society*, Cambridge: Cambridge University Press.
—— (1983) *Local Knowledge*, New York: Basic Books.
—— (1984) 'Anti-antirelativism', *American Anthropologist* 86(2): 263–78.
Gellner, E. (1985) *Relativism and Social Sciences*. Cambridge: Cambridge University Press.
Herbert, C. (1991) *Cuture and Anomie: Ethnographic Imagination in the Nineteenth Century*. Chicago: Chicago University Press.
Kluckhohn C. and Kroeber, A.L. (1963) *Culture: A Critical Review of Concepts and Definitions*, New York: Vintage Books.
Kuper, A. (1994) 'Culture, identity and the project of a cosmopolitan anthropology', *Man*, 29(3): 537–54.
Le Goff, J. and Nora, P. (eds) (1974) *Faire de l'histoire*, Paris: Gallimard.
Leopold, J. (1980) *Culture in Comparative and Evolutionary Perspective: E. B. Tylor and the Making of Primitive Culture*, Berlin: Reiner.
MacIntyre, A. (1981) *After Virtue*, Notre Dame: University of Notre Dame Press.
Malighetti, R. (1991) *Le filosofo e il confesore: Antropologia e ermeneutica in Clifford Geertz*, Milan: Edizioni Unicopli.
Marcus, E.G. (ed.) (1992) *Rereading Cultural Anthropology*, Durham, NC: Duke University Press.
Mari, G. (1986) *Moderno e postmoderno: Soggetto, tempo, sapere nella società attuale*, Milan: Feltrinelli.

Pasquinelli, C. (1985) 'Alla ricerca del moderno', in Bruno Accarino *et al.* (eds), *Sulla Modernità*, Milan: Franco Angeli, pp. 11–14.
—— (1988) 'Il posto della tradizione', in P.S. Adler *et al.* (eds), *Modernizzazione*, Milan: Franco Angeli, pp. 7–86.
Rabinow, P. (1986) 'Representations are social facts: modernity and post-modernity in anthropology', in J. Clifford and G. Marcus (eds), *Writing Culture: The Poetics and Politics of Ethnography*, Berkeley and Los Angeles: University of California Press.
Remotti, F. (1990) *Noi, primitivi: Lo specchio della antropologia*, Turin: Bolati Boringhieri.
Rossi, Paolo (1989) *Paragone degli ingegni moderni e postmoderni*, Bologna: Mulino.
Rossi, Pietro (1970) *Il concetto di cultura*, Torino: Einaudi.
Said, E.W. (1978) *Orientalism*, New York: Random House.
Stocking, G.W. (1968) *Race, Culture and Evolution: Essays in the History of Anthropology*, New York: Free Press.
Taylor, C. (1989) *Sources of Self: The Making of Modern Identity*, Cambridge, Mass.: Harvard University Press.
Thornton, R. (1992) 'The Rhetoric of Ethnographic Holism', in E.G. Marcus (ed.) *Rereading Cultural Anthropology*, Durham, NC: Duke University Press, pp. 15–33.
Tylor, E.B. (1871) *Primitive Culture*, 2 vols,. London: John Murray.
—— (1951) *Primitive Culture*, New York: Harper.
Vattimo, G. (1985) *La fine della modernità*, Milan: Garzanti.
—— (1989) *La società trasparente*, Milan: Garzanti.
Wagner, R. (1975) *The Invention of Culture*, Chicago: University of Chicago Press.

Chapter 5

Circumscribing the environment
Sustainable development, ethnography and applied anthropology in southern Africa

Tim Quinlan

INTRODUCTION

The changing political landscapes of Europe and South Africa may illustrate a universal phenomenon, but there is a palpable North–South divide in anthropological debate on the subject. While postmodernity informs debate and analysis in Europe and North America, a modernist agenda pervades South African debate in support of the proclaimed political drive for a unitary state. Despite the fragmentation of society, the South African Communist Party vies with the Pan African Congress to present itself as a political vanguard. And one cannot forget that 'One nation – One Culture' was a common populist slogan in the early 1990s.

Furthermore, the debates on postmodernism in the North accentuate the apparent parochialism of South African anthropology (Gordon and Spiegel 1993). Yet the underlying ethos of anthropology in South Africa is that that it should be a practical and relevant discipline, involving engaged rather than distanced analysis of society in southern Africa. Postmodernism, therefore, seems to be a luxury affordable amongst North American academes and, perhaps, along the corridors of Cambridge (Strathern 1987). Even if anthropologists in South Africa are generally repelled by crass interventions (Crapanzano 1985), they cannot ignore the influence of anthropologists in the North, be it the mesmerising words of Comaroff (1985) or the seemingly arcane North American fascination with Bushmen (Lee and Guenther 1991; Wilmsen 1989; Wilmsen and Denbow 1990), which manage to cast doubt amongst South African anthropologists about local endeavours (Gordon and Spiegel 1993). This chapter explores this doubt and the antagonism of South African anthropology to its metropolitan well-spring.

The vehicle for discussion is rural environmental research and its evolution in southern Africa under the aegis of 'sustainable development', a concept which emanated in the North and which has been propagated worldwide (Hopper 1988; IUCN 1980; Lebel and Kane 1991; Redclift 1984). Two themes are examined. First, anthropological concern with reflexivity is used to appraise the logic of sustainable development. On the one hand, sustainable development is often an imposition on rural society, that revitalises preservationist ideology by making conservation a commodity, such as in the development of eco-tourism. On the other hand, there is a postmodernist thread in sustainable development, which is expressed in the demand for a plurality of voices in environmental management, and a relativist perspective in terms of accepting the specificity of conditions in a project area, and commonly espoused in terms of 'community participation'. Second, the discussion endorses applied anthropological research as a means for the discipline to appraise its future. This approach is in contrast to the apparent use of postmodernism in France and Britain as a foil, to justify anthropology as a distinctive social science, by recourse to higher and higher levels of theoretical abstraction about the anthropological enterprise.[1] This opposition reflects a long contest in anthropology of which the debate on postmodernism is the most recent outbreak (Carrithers 1990; Friedman 1991; Pool 1991; Sangren 1988), but which can be traced to the origins of twentieth-century anthropology (Clifford 1988: 24–54; Strathern 1987).

The perspective adopted here is that applied research places the anthropologist in a context which challenges the intellectual and ethical ideals of anthropological research, and which is appropriate, therefore, for reassessment of the discipline as a whole. Environmental research in South Africa is used to illustrate this perspective, for it is an arena into which anthropologists have been drawn by a host of interrelated developments, such as the rise of a Green movement; the placement of environmental issues on the national political agendas; the linking of claims to land, and its protection, to ethnic identities; and through the participation of anthropologists in Environmental Impact Assessment (EIA) studies and in debates on environmental policy.

ANTHROPOLOGY AND SUSTAINABLE DEVELOPMENT

The quest for sustainable development is gaining popularity in southern Africa. Much of the attention is on rural areas, such that anthropologists are often called upon to explore the implications of the concept, usually through participation in EIA studies. EIA studies are, in principle, attempts to predict the course of ecological processes in a locality, following the intervention of a development project, and to provide reasoned assessment of the consequences for society. The value of contributing anthropological expertise is often clouded, however, by lack of clarity about the authority of researchers in the studies, the political agendas of clients and study steering committees, and assumptions about the relationship between socio-economic and natural scientific research. In other words, from the start to finish of an EIA study, the 'environment' in question is often circumscribed in ways that the anthropologist finds incompatible with EIA ideals, and with the tenets of anthropological research. This has lead some of us (Boersema and Higgins 1991; Quinlan 1993a, 1993b) to consider whether anthropologists can improve EIA research design in South Africa.

Questioning of EIA practices begins with a critique of the ways in which ecological processes are reified on the basis of the categorisations employed by the different disciplines involved in a study; a common sociological one being presumption that residents in a project locality constitute a community. Yet critique cannot ignore the fact that human intervention to transform environments inevitably involves construction of boundaries around phenomena. In other words, EIA studies are attempts to reconstruct understanding of society and nature, but, in practice, they usually replicate established constructs through use of standard, disciplinary-based, procedures. A result is that such studies do not actually stimulate new knowledge of the dynamics of ecological processes.

It is this contradiction between endeavour to redefine the conceptual division between society and nature, and the inability to do so in practice, which stimulates reflection on anthropology's possible contributions within, and beyond, the confines of environmental research. Although the result of environmental research is often a simplistic redrawing of boundaries around phenomena, the way in which it is done, and the contests amongst and between 'development/ conservation experts' and their 'subjects', lies at the root of anthropological interest. These social dynamics not only illustrate the way social frameworks and ideological boundaries are continually refashioned, but they also provide a sound antidote to essentialist perspectives on society and nature.

I outline this argument through reference to a conservation project in Lesotho and to South Africa's policy for environmental research and management. The project is an intergovernmental programme to implement a conservation policy in the Maluti mountains of Lesotho. The policy in question is South Africa's Integrated Environmental Management (IEM) policy (Council for the Environment 1989a, 1989b; Department of Environmental Affairs 1992) which provides guidelines for EIA studies, and for implementation of development projects.

CONSERVATION MANAGEMENT IN LESOTHO

The eastern ranges of the Maluti mountains are now the focus of a conservation policy which stems from the Drakensberg/Maluti Catchment Conservation Programme (D/MCCP), and United States of America International Development (USAID) support for 'range management' of the region. The D/MCCP was proposed in 1983 during a period of *détente* between Lesotho and South Africa. However, political disputes between these countries delayed implementation of the proposal until 1987. The D/MCCP involved multidisciplinary research which was funded by the South African Department of Foreign Affairs, coordinated by a parastatal conservation agency, the Natal Parks Board (NPB), and carried out mainly by South African based researchers.[2] It also involved officials from Lesotho's Ministry of Agriculture, notably personnel from the Range Management Division which is funded by USAID and partially managed by American personnel.

The start of the D/MCCP was marked by lack of coordination. The field researchers had terms of reference for their particular subprojects, but little idea of the broader intentions of the sponsors and coordinators. The latter had clear, though partially veiled, plans, but no specific procedures for integration of the different subprojects. One outcome was that the study area was eventually demarcated by an ecologist who, in the absence of clear guidelines, surmised the focus on the alpine zone and drew a boundary along the 2,750 m contour line – the standard reference for alpine zoning in this region. This act facilitated research, but at the cost of limiting research on the interconnections between ecological processes within, and beyond, the alpine zone. None the less, the programme provided valuable information on ecological processes in the mountains, for little research has been carried out in this area in the past (Dobb 1985; Staples and Hudson 1938).

However, many of the central conclusions of the field researchers, and their qualifications about the research, were ultimately overridden by the coordinators at the final workshop to design a conservation policy. On the one hand, the Natal Parks Board wanted to ensure that the natural resources of the alpine zone were preserved. The escarpment forms the border between Lesotho and South Africa. Although the NPB has a string of nature reserves along the slopes of the escarpment, it was interested in extending its influence into the area beyond the border and the escarpment. That interest had been declared previously, in the proposal by the International Union for the Conservation of Nature and Natural Resources (IUCN) for the Drakensberg–Maluti escarpment and its environs to be proclaimed as a 'world heritage site' (IUCN 1980), following lobbying by the NPB. On the other hand, USAID personnel sought to integrate the NPB concerns with the efforts of Lesotho's Range Management Division (RMD) to restructure livestock and grazing management practices in the country, through the creation of 'range management areas' (RMAs). The project called for creation of demarcated areas within which rotational grazing schemes could be implemented and managed solely for those residents who had been thus circumscribed.

Both sets of interests supported government and business concerns about the multibillion rand Lesotho Highland Water Project which involves construction of several hydro-electric dams in the mountain region. A particular concern was to minimise soil erosion in the alpine valleys which serve as water catchment areas for the dams. Consequently, the final workshop of the D/MCCP proposed that the original study area be defined as a 'managed resource area' (MRA), on the basis of these concerns rather than through close reference to the programme's research results. In other words, the MRA is a product of mutually reinforcing, national and international, business and conservation interests.

The USAID's RMA project is now foundering on the contradictions between its stated aim to improve livestock production and grassland management for the benefit of Basotho stock owners, and its support of broader political and economic interests. First, the approach reifies the notion of community by reducing it to a territorial entity. The elision began with presumption of the existence of community, through regular use of the term by researchers and officials to describe the common livestock and grazing management practices of Basotho stock owners. This presumption was then confirmed by the demarcation of RMAs, which drew boundaries around villages, villagers and the natural resources they commonly use. Having demarcated the 'environment' in these terms, a stated aim to stimulate local management of resources, in accordance with the principles of 'sustainable development', was inevitably couched in terms of 'community participation' (Artz 1993).

Each RMA is currently managed by officials of the Lesotho government and USAID officials, but grazing associations of residents in each area have been established as the basis for future management.

Second, the logic of the RMA project set up a circular argument. It hid a premise to create community in the sense of developing common effort and shared values amongst rural residents to use the grasslands in the manner prescribed by development agencies. The difficulty of actually doing such a thing, and the possibility of questioning such social engineering was mitigated by emphasising the supposed existence of community in the first place. Furthermore, this logic removed from consideration doubts about scientific ability to foresee the numerous social consequences of changing livestock and grazing management practices. By implanting the idea of the objective existence of community, the implication was that all changes would occur only within this framework. Therefore, the framework would not be substantially altered. Therefore, there was little reason for doubt.

Third, the project has largely ignored the fact that the conservation policy, as a human intervention in a particular context, is both a product of, and catalyst for, ecological change. This is to say it is a particular manifestation of contemporary efforts to diversify the capitalist economy in the region. In this case, part of the rationale for conservation is to improve livestock production, notably the quality of merino and mohair for international markets, amidst a host of other considerations (e.g. the tourism potential of conservation areas; revenue from sale of electricity generated by the hydro-electric scheme; broadening of southern Africa's electricity network). On the one hand, the policy promotes characteristics of the political economy, notably, class formation amongst the target population, and, hence, divisions in society that contradict offical presumptions of social homogeneity in that population. On the other hand, by contributing to development of new ecological dynamics (e.g. revision of livestock management to improve quality of the product; introduction of tourism), the policy stimulates forces of a complexity that cannot possibly be contained within its spatial framework.

This short critique illustrates some of the dynamics of human interaction with the environment which are ignored in Lesotho's conservation programmes. The problem is one of prescribing social frameworks without acknowledging that the act of intervention is not only based on simplistic modelling of existing dynamics, but also sets in motion changes which confound those prescriptions. In other words, the matrix of interactions within rural settlements, and between the proponents of the conservation policy and rural residents, may be described very generally as a struggle over what the social order should be in rural Lesotho. The dynamics of this dialectical process are evident in the thought and actions of those directly involved in the implementation of the conservation policy.

First, the creation of RMAs has drawn attention to the ever-changing means by which Basotho classify and use natural resources. With regard to livestock, Basotho employ a transhumance system. In order to protect cultivated fields in village environs, livestock are sent to the mountain grasslands away from villages during summer months. Herders stay with the livestock throughout the summer, living in rough stone shelters known as *metebo* (grazing posts).[3] After harvest time, livestock are brought down to graze on grassland in village environs. This system evolved in the colonial context of the late nineteenth century as Basotho settled in the mountain region, but it is based on a pre-colonial ethos. The ethos is that land, like air and water, is fundamental to human survival and hence, inalienable. This ethos gave rise to usufructuary principles of land tenure, and differentiation of natural products of the land as resources to be exploited according to their availability and the demands of users.

The principle of usufruct remains the basis of land tenure in Lesotho, but numerous distinctions in types and uses of land have evolved as Basotho contended, with social developments, in the twentieth century, such as population growth within a finite territory, and development of a market economy in livestock amidst increasing dependence of people on remitted migrant wage earnings (Murray 1981; Phororo 1979; Quinlan 1984; Spiegel 1979). Figure 5.1 presents the current classification of resources, and indicates the interweaving of the main categorisations which arose from the need of rural Basotho to reconstruct their relationship with the land as economic circumstances change.

In principle, all natural resources are communal resources but individuals have right of use and security of tenure to some resources, notably the fields allocated to them and their residential sites. Trees can now be both a communal resource, whose use is dictated by chiefs, and private property (e.g. fruit trees planted by an individual). The principle of usufruct is expressed in use of the singular form of the word for communal resources (*maboella*, sg. *leboella*) to mean that use is restricted in some way, for a particular purpose. A chief may reserve an area (*letobo*), for example, for use by certain animals for certain periods. Likewise, restrictions on use of grasslands in village environs

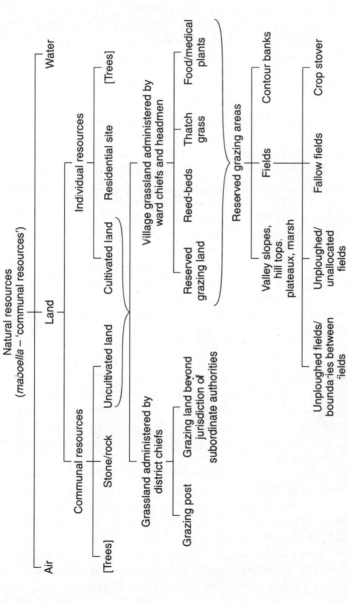

Figure 5.1 Contemporary classification of land resource categories in Lesotho

Source: Revision of Shoup 1987; 26–7

change regularly during a year. Cultivated fields are always defined as *leboella* during summer months, meaning that livestock are prohibited from them, but then redefined as communal grazing land for the duration of winter. Yet fields not under cultivation may be opened for communal grazing during summer months, for animals that are used daily, and have to be kept in the villages, such as milch cows and horses.

The RMA project has appropriated the criterion of use – grassland as grazing land – and sought to isolate it as a discrete category through imposition of the American word, 'range'. The intervention ignores the way grassland is currently defined in Sesotho. First, Sesotho categorisations refer primarily to the type of grass and its location. Built into the categorisation is recognition of the biolgical character-istics of different grasses, such as their growth patterns, which are used to determine potential uses. The potential uses are differentiated such that use of grassland for grazing livestock is subject to the demand on grassland for other purposes. Second, livestock require access to many of the designated *maboella* resources and therefore, grazing land/ 'range' falls into a number of resource categories.

There is clearly a wide discrepancy between government officials' and stock owners' understanding of livestock and grassland manage-ment. The irony of the situation is that neither perspective resolves the question of how to prevent environmental degradation. Although the government officials are informed by theoretical constructs such as sustainable development, in practice they adopt a narrow strategy; to excise the natural resource under threat, and then to focus on the question of how to protect it. In contrast, stock owners acknowledge the many pressures emanating beyond the grazing areas which threaten their abilities to rear livestock. In turn, they adopt an equally narrow strategy which is to protect their livestock, even if it is a cost to natural resources in some localities.

The grassland has been circumscribed by expansion of settlements and geopolitical boundaries. The development of the market economy in livestock products, particularly wool and mohair, has promoted accumulation of livestock. Increasing use of land in village environs for arable farming has reduced acreages available for use as grazing land. Increase in numbers of livestock kept in villages during summer months has reduced the quality and quantity of forage for use in winter. As a result of these pressures, Basotho have begun to modify the transhumance system. With less forage available in villages, stock owners have begun to establish 'winter' grazing posts. This is a recent development which was initiated about fifteen years ago. 'Winter' grazing posts are located in sub-alpine valleys within 3 to 4 hours' walk from villages and stock owners use them intensively during winter. The establishment of these winter posts is having profound effects.

First, changes to livestock management strategies have altered seasonal livestock movement and livestock density patterns. 'Winter' grazing posts are used as a solution to the combined problems of finding adequate forage and minimising the hazards of rearing livestock in a cold climate and harsh terrain. The posts are occupied at the onset of winter in June. Stock owners move their animals (cattle, sheep, goats, donkeys, horses) to and from these posts according to changes in the weather and capability of particular breeds and species to withstand cold climatic conditions. Sheep and horses, for example, may be kept at these posts even when snow falls (as long as the snow does not lie for more than 2 to 3 days), but other animal species will be removed to the villages at the first sign of impending snow. Come spring, the animals are brought back to the posts in accordance with increase in mean temperatures. Ewes, lambs and horses are the first to be sent to these posts, followed by cattle and donkeys and, finally, when there is no threat of frost and snow, by (goat) does and kids. Rams and bucks are generally kept in villages all year, as in the past, in order to control conception. They are usually brought up to the 'winter' grazing posts in July to cover the ewes and does, and to ensure birth of lambs and kids in September and October, respectively.

Second, the establishment of 'winter' posts has brought into question the division of authority between district and ward (and sub-ward) chiefs over grassland. A territorial base to the authority of chiefs was endorsed during the colonial era such that for each district there is one district chief, and below this office there are a number of ward and sub-ward chiefs who have jurisdiction over specific territories. These latter areas were drawn in relation to settlements such that non-settlement areas, notably the high mountain valleys were excluded from the jurisdiction of the ward and sub-ward chiefs. Accordingly, authority over these highland areas fell to the district chief, and it is to this office that people go, as in the past, to get permisssion to build grazing-posts. The outcome was that district chiefs came to be regarded as authorities over grazing-post areas. The problem now is that people are establishing their 'winter' grazing posts in valleys within, and on the borders of, the ward and sub-ward chiefs' areas of jurisdiction. The potential for contest of authority in this context is evident, as the use and number of 'winter' posts increases.

Third, accelerated soil erosion and degradation of vegetation is far more extensive in the environs of the 'winter' grazing-posts than in the 'summer' grazing post areas. This is due generally to the location of 'winter' grazing posts in tributary valleys which are comparatively narrower, warmer and drier than the larger alpine valleys used during summer months. Accordingly, stock densities are often greater in the tributary valleys while the temperature regime of these valleys makes the soils susceptable to accelarated erosion when disturbed (Morris and Quinlan 1994).

A particular fault with Lesotho's conservation management policy is its failure to take into account these ecological processes, even though they were were voiced during the D/MCCP. The evasion is due to the politics of conservation which were underwritten in this context by South African and international conservationists' interest in the Drakensberg/Maulti escarpment as a 'world heritage site'. This interest in an area which is generally regarded as an 'alpine area' was inevitably translated by the D/MCCP's natural scientists in the field according to their definition of 'alpine' grassland. The 2,750 masl (metres above sea level) contour line was the obvious means for demarcation of the study area. However, the stated concern to protect the 'alpine area' was invalidated by the ecologists' more rigorous distinctions in terms of the lack of degradation in the 'Alpine belt' and evident degradation in the upper 'Sub-Alpine belt' (Morris, Boleme and Tainton 1991) (see Figure 5.2).

There is virtually no degradation in the Alpine belt because herders rarely graze their animals at this altitude. The grasses are not palatable to livestock; stock owners know that the grasses have little forage value; and herders do not like the arduous work involved in keeping track of livestock on the steep slopes and amongst the crags where livestock can easily become lost. Instead, livestock are grazed on the lower slopes which fall within the ecologists' category, Sub-Alpine belt. The distinction is an academic nicety, which does not override the legitimacy of observation of degradation and concern about it, however the location is defined, be it in terms of natural scientists' categories or popular sentiment of the area as a unique geographical phenomenon.

None the less, use of the 2,750 masl contour line to demarcate the study area ensured that the upper Sub-Alpine belt was included within the ambit of the ecologists' studies. This line simply marks the approximate division between the Alpine and Sub-Alpine belts. The ecologists recognised that the boundaries of their categories could only be drawn adequately in relation to observation of local conditions. In

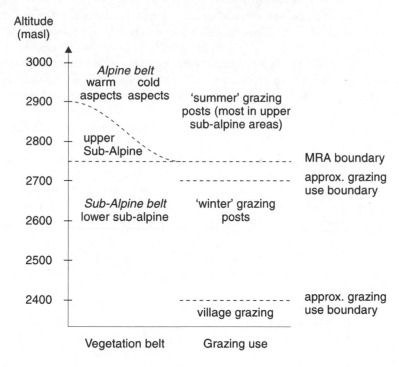

Figure 5.2 Alpine belt and Sub-Alpine belt categorisations and grazing-post areas

the Drakensberg/Maluti region, the division between the categories is defined largely in relation to the different temperature regimes on north-facing (warm) and on south-facing (cold) slopes (see Figure 5.2). The study area managed to include 'sub-alpine' grassland which was observably being degraded (Morris, Boleme and Tainton 1991), and thus provided evidence to support the conservationists' concerns.

In a further ironic twist, the emprical rigour of natural science research from which it draws authority, prevented presentation of the greater danger of degradation in the lower Sub-Alpine belt. The ecologists' research suggested that if the grassland of the upper zone was being degraded, so too was the grassland in lower zone, and this hypothesis was supported by anthropological research on use of 'winter' grazing posts (Morris and Quinlan 1994). The findings could only be presented as a strong impression, however, for the ecologists could do little research outside the study area and, therefore, they could not present findings authoritatively.[4] The outcome was inevitable. The findings were ignored at the final D/MCCP workshop because they lacked 'authority'. They could not, indeed, be accepted without bringing into the open the political reasons for demarcation of the MRA, which have less to do with stock owners' problems than with the concerns of the NPB and the IUCN.

A consequence of the D/MCCP is that the problem of grassland degradation has been circumvented. While the conservationists justifiably emphasise livestock as a cause of grassland degradation, they ignore stock owners' reasons for placing primary emphasis on their livestock. Likewise, the stock owners' justifiable emphasis on livestock is at a cost of considering the physical consequences in the long term to the grassland. Yet it is not as if stock owners have ignored the concerns voiced by conservationists in the past and today. Rather, the different emphases reflect a struggle waged by rural residents to mediate collective and individual interests in the face of the many pressures on rural livelihoods.

The conservation policy ignores the fact that Basotho cannot afford to excise resources, either conceptually or in practice, in the manner demanded by government officials and their sponsors. They live in knowledge of environmental degradation as a process, and take into account the many causes in their efforts to maintain livestock. The circumstances are such that they are being constrained on all sides. Job opportunities for migrants are diminishing in South Africa, which, in turn, places greater demands on rural resources. Likewise, the development of wool and mohair markets, and recent inception of beef-marketing facilities, means that livestock are increasingly a vital commodity to offset endemic poverty in the rural areas. In response, rural residents seek to protect what is to them a critical resource, namely, livestock.

These tensions are manifested in current livestock management practices wherein collective, mutual support contends with individual desperation. Most stock owners, for example, have few animals, such that many combine their herds with friends or kin. Often one party will provide the grazing post while the other(s) provide a young agnate to herd the livestock. In a different vein, the struggle between collective and individual interest is evident in responses to problems of finding adequate winter forage. For instance, the crop stover in harvested fields is, in principle, forage for communal use but nowadays individuals often remove stover from their own fields for use as fodder for their own livestock.[5]

In view of these developments, the commitment of the conservationists to 'community participation' seems facile. The principles of communal tenure have been transformed in the past, as a result of rural investment in the market potential of livestock. Today, the creation of 'winter' grazing posts and invention of 'range' are indications of another transformation in which principles and practices of livestock and grazing management are being redefined. This has lead to recategorisation of natural resources, and hence, to redrawing of the 'environment', all of which impinge on the way community is expressed in rural Lesotho. Already there are conflicting dynamics of which stock owners, if not the conservationists, are aware.

Rotational grazing schemes and grazing associations, for example, are of greater value to wealthy stock owners than to the majority who own few livestock. If one has sizeable herds, and can afford to employ a number of herders, it is relatively easy to accommodate official stipulations on rotational grazing. Moreover, it is in the interests of wealthy stock owners to adopt these procedures because, as stock owners have learnt from interventions during the colonial era (Basutoland Government 1920, 1954; Department of Agriculture 1938; Phororo 1979), rotational grazing is necessary to sustain large herds. For the majority who have small herds, rotational grazing is seen to be unnecessary because they know that the grassland in the environs of their grazing posts has supported their animals in the past, and seems capable of doing so in the future. With regard to grazing associations, the membership fees are not substantial to the wealthy individual, but are costly to the poorer stock owner. Similarly, even though the associations provide services such as access to stud animals, the unit cost is less for the person who has a large herd than for one who has a few animals.

On a more general level, the authority of chiefs over use of grasslands is being challenged by the conservation policy. If the policy is enforced in the future, it would not be surprising to see a system of grazing management dictated by officials supported by wealthy stock owners who promote market-based relationships in livestock management. The majority of stock owners, whose practices, as much as their opportunities to rear livestock, are questioned by the MRA and by RMAs, are already showing resistance. They rely on the authority of chiefs to articulate a communal approach to livestock and grazing management. As in the past, public meetings are held to decide when and where people may graze livestock. The most important meetings occur in spring, to decide when to prohibit use of village grassland and 'winter' grazing-post areas. These meetings involve lengthy debate on environmental risks. These include current and potential weather conditions (kids are particularly susceptible to cold; the need for cattle as draft power to plough and sow fields depends on when the rains fall), the condition of winter grazing relative to spring growth of grasses on summer pastures, and the general forage requirements of livestock. Chiefs make the decisions, but after popular consensus has been reached, and the voice of the majority who own few animals is the most powerful.

In summary, current environmental research and management in Lesotho highlights efforts by those involved to create a social order compatible with perceived contemporary and future economic conditions. The focus is on the present and the future, but the outcome is by no means clearly discernible. The interaction amongst rural residents, and between themselves and conservation agencies, is a dialectical process. Subjective aspirations are offset by the objective implications of particular interventions which, in turn, are modified by the particular ways in which people respond to them.

The discussion here has highlighted the disposition of the conservationists to dictate to rural Basotho an understanding of the environment, which employs reified concepts, but which also illustrates social boundaries in the making. The competition to define these boundaries illustrates their continual redefinition through what is, in effect, a dialogue between conservationists and rural residents. For the anthropologist, the limitations of this dialogue, the evident effort to transcend them as they become apparent, and the shifting power differentials between those involved, must inevitably demand reconsideration of the concepts used to explain these dynamics. This means doubting neither the utility of concepts like community, nor anthropological authority to explain social developments. Rather, the complexity of the interactions and interventions demands that which has become axiomatic in anthropology, namely, reflexivity. In a context of engaged research, this means alertness to the way in which concepts are used, and awareness of the discord and/or concord between the boundaries that are presumed in their use. With regard to anthropological authority, it is precisely the context of applied research which demonstrates the importance of developing a sound basis to command authority. The necessary shift in research perspectives is suggested in contemporary thinking on sustainable development. As I discuss below, however, the implications for environmental research and management, let alone for anthropology, have yet to be fully acknowledged in South Africa.

ENVIRONMENTAL MANAGEMENT AND APPLIED
ANTHROPOLOGY IN SOUTH AFRICA

The imposition of conservationists' concepts upon the subjects of development projects, and the inequalities in the dialogue between them, are obvious foci for analysis by anthropologists who participate in applied research. Yet it is also inevitable that a critical analysis must raise personal doubts about the value of applied anthropological research. My argument may be summarised as follows. Involvement in applied research begins usually with a critique of policy and procedures. The critique demonstrates, at one level, the value of anthropology by questioning the logic of multidisciplinary environmental research, and, notably, the perspectives of the natural sciences. Yet such critique also compels the anthroplogist to initiate an auto-critique, challenging the familiarity of common sociological concepts which he or she uses to explain events, and to criticise those of other disciplines. This leads to questioning the scope and boundaries of anthroplogy as a discipline, because the imperative to create new knowledge of ecological processes demands exploration of ways to integrate different disciplines. The outcome is an immersion for anthropology in the natural sciences, from which the discipline can emerge as a different discipline certainly, but also more capable of providing insight into ecological processes and human understanding about them.

In South Africa, environmental research and management is governed largely by the current IEM policy (Council for the Environment 1989a, 1989b; Department of Environmental Affairs 1992). The documents are a systematic attempt to guide research by encouraging EIA studies, and by showing how they should be designed. For instance, the policy was introduced in the following terms:

> On one level, this document describes a way of thinking about environmental management that reconciles the disparate demands of conservation and development. On another level, the document prescribes a set of operational guidelines – or a 'code of practice' – directed at finding that elusive balance between conservation and development, the goal of which is to make progress sustainable and improve the quality of life for all South Africa's peoples.
>
> (Council for the Environment 1989a: 1)

The importance of understanding ecological processes in dialectical terms is subsequently highlighted:

These procedures which are interactive and iterative in nature, stimulate creative thinking in the planning and initial design stage, provide a systematic approach to evaluation and the evolution of proposals in the assessment stage, formalize the approval process in the decision making stage, and ensure that monitoring and desirable modifications take place in the implementation stage.

(Council for the Environment 1989a: 4)

As I have discussed in detail elsewhere (Quinlan 1993a, 1993b), the policy, and the recently refined EIA procedures, emphasise the need to establish dialogue between researchers, project proponents and project subjects. The procedures seek to express the principles of sustainable development, as enunciated by the proponents of the World Conservation Strategy (WCS) (Hanks 1986; Hopper 1988; IUCN 1980; IUCN, UNEP and WWF 1991; Lebel and Kane 1990), which, in summary, are the need to pool resources (skills and means), for collaboration, for ongoing research, and to educate (to change attitudes and practices). The aims of the policy and of EIA studies are contradicted, however, by a logic which predetermines the scope for dialogue. Briefly put, the contradiction lies in reliance on existing structures of environmental research and management. The policy assumes that IEM and EIA studies can be implemented under the aegis of existing local and regional, government and parastatal authorities without any change in the relationship between them and the populace. The improbability of maintaining the *status quo* has been highlighted, however, by the successes and problems encountered by a growing number of locality based 'sustainable development' projects in southern Africa (Fig 1991; Jacobsohn 1991; Lawson 1991; Murombedzi 1992; Zimbabwe Trust 1990).

Similarly, the quest to see ecological processes in dialectical terms is negated by a presumption that changes to socioeconomic conditions and to the condition of natural resources can be analysed from within existing disciplinary boundaries for research. The promise for 'integration' of different scientific disciplines is abrogated by procedures which promote compartmentalised, multi-disciplinary research. The opportunity for cross-fertilisation of ideas and findings is lost as each writes a report from within the confines of his or her own discipline. To make the compilation of a final report easier, the researchers are often required to reduce their respective insights to quantifiable artifices; change expressed as impact, and mitigation, as the application of a force to counter undesirable effects, and to encourage desirable effects.

What is seen to be desirable and undesirable, is subject to the hierarchy of power built into the organisation of EIA studies. Decisions rest ultimately upon consensus amongst a distanced steering committee. The tacit implication that the researchers should be involved in the planning and design of a project, openly suggested in the encouragement to consider alternative options for a project, becomes lost in a contradiction; the researchers are included in a research programme after a conservation/development agency has produced a detailed proposal, and after the EIA steering committee has defined the scope for dialogue amongst all who are involved. Underlying this situation in South Africa is the relative pre-eminence and authority of the physical and natural sciences. Given that the authority of the researchers to influence decisions is constrained at the start, so too is participation in the process by the subjects – the 'affected parties'.

For most EIA researchers, unease about these constraints highlights the palpable gap between intent and practice. The anthropologist can take little comfort in the apparent confirmation of disdain for applied research amongst peers in the North. There are good reasons for this disdain given the litany of failure of 'development' in the South. However, it is a safe stance which verges on retreat from confronting the reality of social contexts in which many anthropologists work. Whatever the focus of academic anthropological studies, the socio-economic context is more than likely today to include social processes emanating from some form of 'development' intervention. In the field of environmental research, gobal interest in sustainable development offers an opportunity to confront these processes. However uncertain the utility of the concept of sustainable development may seem, and despite its manipulation by powerful international and national agencies, what occurs in its name, and the questions that confront researchers, provides the anthropologist not only the opportunity for objective critique but also for reassessment of the discipline's endeavours.

The recent creation of the Richtersveld National Park in Namaqualand is an apt illustration. The park circumscribes land used by stock farmers who used to be legally categorised as 'coloured', and who occupy what was once a designated 'coloured reserve' (Balic 1990; Fig 1991). Anthropologists have been involved in the multi-layered conflicts arising from the state's intention to create the park and use of the concept of sustainable development to guide research and negotiations. The park has been established, and, currently, to the satisfaction of the residents. The research and the negotiations involved the residents of the Richtersveld, residents in neighbouring 'coloured reserves', environmentalists, other scientists, political authorities and, at one stage, the state funding body for social science research, in a process which generally pitted the state against the rest (Boonzaier 1991). None the less, the lines of allegiance and opposition have rarely settled, and they continue to shift (Archer 1991). While some researchers of different disciplines have combined scholarly and advocacy roles, the experience has drawn residents, activists and academic scholars together in ways which have lead them to reconsider their perspectives not only on environmental management, but also on the politics and social dynamics of ethnic identity (Sharp and Boonzaier 1993; Stein 1992).

In southern Africa, disciplinary boundaries are being crossed, and distinctions between academic and applied research are becoming blurred, in an increasing number of environmental research pro-grammes. There is little coherency in these enquiries, given that they are largely experimental and have yet to be systematically debated, but this seems to be the case generally. Natural scientists have begun to question orthodoxy in their own disciplines (Norse 1987), to reassess research procedures (Ellis 1989) and to recognise the limitations of quantitative modelling which stem from the bias towards using the methodologies of the natural and physical sciences as a framework for applied environmental research (Starfield and Bleloch 1991). However fragmented the interventions and debates may be, a common thread is emerging. In one word, it is dialogue. Dialogue is the concern at every level of environmental research, be it policy dictation, 'grass-roots' intervention, multi-disciplinary EIA studies, or researchers' internal debates about the capabilities of their own disciplines.

There are, of course, many nuances in the way dialogue is being expressed. For policy-makers and project managers, dialogue is often a veiled attempt to legitimate development projects. The notion of dialogue is also the basis for criticism of environmental policies and EIA study design, as is illustrated in the preceding section. Dialogue also lies at the core of the researchers' doubts about their involvement in applied research, and in reassessments of their own disciplines. The principle of dialogue implies that the subjects of a project may be brought 'on board' as authors of a development project, but it also establishes a basis for the subjects to question the authority of those who seek their participation, and the terms on which they are supposed to participate. For anthropologists in particular, dialogue is the key to making sense of the complex dynamics of environmental research, even though their position, betwixt project managers and the subjects may seem untenable.

The applied aspect of their work requires establishment of a research framework that encourages the participation of a project's subjects, but also subtly forces a project's sponsors and managers to relinquish their authority, and prescribed disciplinary-based research procedures. The analytical aspect of their work draws out the dynamics of the many contradictions in applied research, but, importantly, brings to the fore a hidden protagonist, in the form of the postmodernist debate from the North. On the one hand, the anthropologist is engaged in what seems to be a modernist project, in view of the proclaimed attempt of sustainable development projects towards enlightenment and synchronisation of knowledge. Accordingly, postmodernist thinking is something to be reacted against and rejected. On the other hand, the anthropologist cannot ignore the fact that postmodernism informs their efforts to unravel the dynamics of the circumstances in which they work; notably, the contingency of their authority, and uncertainties about representation of the relationships between policy-makers, researchers and their subjects.

For anyone who has been involved in EIA studies, or so-called 'community'-based conservation projects, the quest for dialogue between the intervening sponsors and local subjects is usually very apparent. If the anthropologist is directly involved in a project, he or she is drawn into playing a mediatory role. This role is, first, to make the sponsors aware of their presumptions and the socio-economic implications of the dialogue which it propagates. Second, the role is to create a dialogue between sponsor and subject that allows them to become aware of the potential changes to society following intervention, and to take responsibility for choosing a particular path. In short, the role is to show that conservation and development is a process of continual transformation of society and its environs.

The current format for environmental research in South Africa may prevent the anthropologist from realising this role, but it cannot prevent realisation that disciplinary boundaries have to be crossed, if the notion of sustainable development is to be of any value in promoting new knowledge of ecological processes. The attempt to promote dialogue, and, indeed, the constraints against it, inevitably show how multi-disciplinary research presupposes divisions within ecological processes, and hence, negates its own aspirations. Dialogue, therefore, must begin with the researchers, and between a researcher and the tenets of his or her own discipline, in order to counter predetermined circumscription of the environment, and to overcome the limitations of particular scientific discourses. This means, for the anthropologist, challenging the procedures and logic of other disciplines involved in the research. In other words, the imperative is to focus attention on the way the subjects and proponents of a project will reshape their understanding of their environment, circumscribing it a different way from the past, and yet be subject in the future to the ecological consequences. Creating this dialogic framework undoubtedly subverts current environmental research procedures, but in that lies optimism for the future of the discipline.

The opportunity lies in the principles of sustainable development which suggest revision of research and management structures, in order to address the specificity of ecological processes in localities. However much current environmental research procedures may reflect an attempt to minimise disruption of existing structures, the challenge for the anthropologist is to contest the bias towards generalisation. The anthropologist can do this, for the particular is precisely the domain in which he or she has expertise. Yet this imperative involves engagement with the natural and physical scientists. By crossing disciplinary boundaries and initiating dialogue, the anthropologist can begin to claim an authority hitherto denied in this field. Such authority may be won with respect to other disciplines, but it is based on confronting the uncertainties about the discipline, which the debate on postmodernism has posed. That confrontation is the internal dialogue of the anthropologist, in which the debate is a valuable resource for engaging with other disciplines, and for using environmental research to broaden the scope of the discipline.

CONCLUSION

I have used global interest in sustainable development, and its interpretations in southern Africa, to explore the apparent intellectual divide between anthropology in South Africa, and in Europe and North America. Setting up a North–South polarity is more than a polemical device. It is really a short-hand way to express some complex dynamics in current debates within the discipline, notably, on postmodernism. On the one hand, it expresses the emergent political division of the world, and its reverberations in the discipline of anthropology. The reverberations include the suspicion of anthropologists in the South about postmodernism, in view of the growing challenge to what is popularly entitled 'Euro-centricism'. On the other hand the polarity indicates subtle changes in a long-standing relationship between the metropolitan source of anthropology and its practice elsewhere in the world.

It is a relationship which sustains the discipline in South Africa. But the relationship is no longer clearly defined, partly as a result of the professional isolation of South African anthropologists for many years, and the attendant problems of parochialism which Gordon and Spiegel (1993) have discussed. An additional factor, however, is the way anthropological research opportunities have been sustained locally through applied work (and likely to continue, in view of the new government's marked use of local intellectual research expertise in the formulation of various policies). Through exploration of anthropological interest in environmental research in southern Africa, I have attempted to explore the impetus of the discipline here, and the changes to its relationship with its metropolitan source. My concern has been not only to highlight the potential contributions of anthropology in the objective effort to understand the dynamics of ecological processes. I have tried to draw out the underlying contexts and implications for anthropologists. Two issues stand out from this discussion.

First, the contexts of anthropological research today are likely to incorporate both conservationist interventions which have immediate, and long-term, consequences on the livelihoods of people in the localities where the anthropologists work, and increasing demands from 'subjects' for anthropologists to demonstrate the utility of their research in some form. Although there is nothing novel about these circumstances, the same cannot be said of anthropologists' contemporary responses to them. As anthropology has grown, and deliberately sought out the complex social dynamics of a rapidly changing and uncertain world, so the responses have become subject to circumstances, partially of their own making, which inevitably inspire reflection upon the foundations and rationale of their endeavours. If this is the basis of the debate on postmodernism in anthropology, it is also the source of suspicion in South African anthropology. What inspires suspicion is introspection which seems to distance anthropologists from the circumstances in which they work.

The second emphasis is exploration of these dynamics of circumstance in terms of the dialogue that they generate. The thrust of the chapter is to disentangle the multi-vocality of the dialogue in which the anthropologist is involved. On the one hand, it is an exposition of anthropologists' ability to show boundaries in the making in the interaction between conservation/development agencies and the subjects of projects, thereby promoting improved insights into ecological processes. In turn, the discussion suggests an optimistic future for anthropology as a subversive discipline, through the ability of anthropologists to engage openly with the circumstances in which they work; in effect, to challenge all and sundry. On the other hand, the focus is an illustration of how disentangling this multivocality is itself an act of redrawing the content and boundaries of the discipline.

The underlying intent of this twofold focus is to draw into the open the hidden protagonist. The debate on postmodernism in anthropology is seductive in suggesting postmodernism in general, as the protagonist. However, the confusion in the debate is enough to indicate this to be an apparition. On the one hand, anthropology has thrived on discovering the particular, the diversity of culture and the transience of social structure, while anthropologists thrive on the uncertainty and contingency of their field experiences. On the other hand, the debate seems to revolve around surprise at the apparent re-emergence of the particular, in reaction to the apparent globalisation of European and North American economic and political hegemony.

The protagonist is really doubt about the discipline's success at explaining the particular. Anthropology actually has a long-standing metaphor for this shadow of doubt; as a problem of collecting butterflies – facts – without always a clear idea of the purpose. The metaphor focused attention on what to do with the facts, ignoring the possibility that the purpose might lie in the act of collecting. Anthropology is a magpie discipline, always finding in the particular, fragments of the unity of humanity. This is what sustains the discipline. The debate on postmodernism may highlight the frustration of dealing with these fragments, but it also encourages the discipline to extend itself beyond current academic confines.

NOTES

1 This is an impression gained at the second conference of the European Association of Social Anthropologists held in Prague, August 1992.
2 I was involved in the D/MCCP as the 'socio-economist' to carry out anthropological research on livestock and grazing management practices of Basotho stock owners and herders.
3 *Motebo* and *metebo* are usually translated in English as 'cattle-post' and 'cattle-posts' respectively. The translation is a misnomer today given that the majority of livestock are merino sheep and angora goats.
4 During research for the D/MCCP an ecologist, Craig Morris, and myself believed that our research data could only support a strong impression that

the focus on the alpine zone was misdirected. During 1991 we followed up our previous research through the Conservation and Livestock Management Project, an integrated project involving coordinated work by ourselves and a video film crew. This project has confirmed our impressions stated in the original D/MCCP.

5 There is not space here to discuss in detail the background to this development. However, the private use of stover is related to change in the land tenure system in which all the products of fields are being seen to be private property as the fields themselves come to be seen as private property. This development is a manifestation of various econonomic and ecological pressures similar to those discussed in this chapter.

REFERENCES

Archer, F. (1991) 'Richtersveld Park, off to a shaky start', *New Ground*, No. 5 (Spring): 47.

Artz, N. (1993) 'Local participation, equity and popular support in Lesotho's Range Management Area programme', *African Journal of Range and Forage Science*, 10(1): 54–62.

Balic, S. (1990) 'Richtersvelders win land rights tug-o-war', *New Ground*, 1(1): 6–7.

Basutoland Government (1920) *Colonial Report: Basutoland*, Pretoria: Government Printer.

—— (1954) *Colonial Report: Basutoland*, Maseru: Comptroller of Stores.

Boersema, N. and G. Higgins, (1991) 'Social impact assessment: the "new" positivism', paper delivered to the Conference for the Association for Anthropology in Southern Africa, 11–14 September, Johannesburg.

Boonzaier, E. (1991) 'People, parks and politics', in M. Ramphele (ed.), *Restoring the Land: Environment and Change in South Africa*, London: Panos, pp. 155–62.

Carrithers, M. (1990) 'Is anthropology art or science?', *Current Anthropology*, 31(3): 263–82.

Clifford, J. (1988) *The Predicament of Culture*, Cambridge, Mass.: Harvard University Press.

Comaroff, J. (1985) *Body of Power, Spirit of Resistance*, Chicago: University of Chicago Press.

Council for the Environment (1989a) *Integrated Environmental Management in South Africa*, Pretoria: Joan Lotter publications.

—— (1989b) *An Approach to a National Environmental Policy and Strategy for South Africa*, Pretoria: Joan Lotter Publications.

Crapanzano, V. (1985) *Waiting: The Whites of South Africa*, New York: Vintage Press.

Department of Agriculture (1938) *Basutoland Department of Agriculture Annual Report*, London: HMSO.

Department of Environmental Affairs (1992) *Integrated Environmental Management Guideline Series*, vols 1–6, Pretoria: Department of Environmental Affairs.

Dobb, A. (1985) 'The organisation of range use in Lesotho, southern Africa: a review of attempted modification and case study', M.Sc. thesis, Washington State University.

Ellis, D. (1989) *Environments at Risk, Case Histories of Impact Assessment*, Berlin: Springer-Verlag.

Fig, D. (1991) 'Flowers in the desert: community struggles in Namaqualand', in J. Cock and E. Koch (eds), *Going Green: People, Politics and the Environment in South Africa*, Cape Town: Oxford University Press, pp. 112–280.

Friedman, J. (1991) 'Further notes on Phallus in Blunderland', in L. Nencel and P. Pels (eds), *Constructing Knowledge*, London: Sage, pp. 95–113.

Gordon, R. and Spiegel, A. (1993) 'Southern Africa revisited', *Annual Review of Anthropology*, 22: 83–105.

Hanks, J. (1986) *Human Populations and the World Conservation Strategy*, Gland: International Union for the Conservation of Nature and Natural Resources.

Hopper, W. (1988) 'The Seventh World Conservation Lecture, the World Bank's challenge: balancing economic need with environmental protection', *The Environmentalist*, 8(2): 165–75.

IUCN (1980) *The World Conservation Strategy*, Gland: International Union for the Conservation of Nature and Natural Resources.

IUCN, UNEP and WWF (1991) *Caring for the Earth: A Strategy for Sustainable Living*, Gland: International Union for the Conservation of Nature and Natural Resources, United Nations Environment Programme and the World Wildlife Fund.

Jacobsohn, M. (1991) 'The crucial link: conservation and development', in J. Cock and E. Koch (eds), *Going Green: People, Politics and the Environment in South Africa*, Cape Town: Oxford University Press, pp. 210–20.

Lawson, L. (1991) 'The ghetto and the greenbelt: the environmental crisis in the urban areas', in J. Cock and E. Koch (eds), *Going Green, People, Politics and the Environment in South Africa*, Cape Town: Oxford University Press, pp. 46–63.

Lebel, G. and Kane, H. (1991) *Sustainable Development: A Guide to our Common Future*, Paris: The Centre for Our Common Future.

Lee, R. and Guenther, M. (1991) 'Oxen or onions? The search for trade (and truth) in the Kalahari', *Current Anthropology*, 32(5): 592–601.

Morris, C. and Quinlan, T. (1994) 'Implications of changes to livestock transhumance for the conservation policy of the mountain catchments of eastern Lesotho', *African Journal of Range and Forage Science*, 11(3): 76–81.

Morris, C., Boleme, T. and Tainton, N. (1991) *Final Report of the Fire and Grazing Project of the Drakensberg/Maluti Catchment Conservation Programme*, Pietermaritzburg: Natal Parks Board.

Murombedzi, J. (1992) 'Decentralising common property resource management: a case study of the Nyaminyami District Council of Zimbabwe's Wildlife Management Programme', Issues Paper No. 30, International Institute for Environment and Development, London.

Murray, C. (1981) *Families Divided*, Johannesburg: Ravan Press.

Norse, E. (1987) 'Habitat diversity and genetic variability: are they necessary ecosystem properties?', in S. Draggon, J. Cohrssen and R. Morrison (eds),

Preserving Ecological Systems: The Agenda for Long Term Research and Development, New York: Praeger, pp. 93–113.

Phororo, D. (1979) *Livestock Farming in Lesotho and Pasture Utilisation*, Maseru: Ministry of Agriculture.

Pool, R. (1991) 'Postmodern anthropology?', *Critique of Anthropology*, 11(4): 309–31.

Quinlan, T. (1984) 'The transformation of land tenure in Lesotho', MA thesis, University of Cape Town.

—— (1993a) 'Environmental impact assessment studies in South Africa: good in principle, poor in practice?', *South African Journal of Science*, 89(3): 106–10.

—— (1993b) 'South Africa's integrated environmental management policy at the crossroads of conservation and development', *Development Southern Africa*, 10(2): 229–38.

Redclift, M. (1984) *Development and the Environmental Crisis*, London: Methuen.

Sangren, P. (1988) 'Rhetoric and the authority of ethnography: "postmodernism" and the social reproduction of texts', *Current Anthropology*, 29(3): 405–35.

Sharp, J. and Boonzaier, E. (1993) 'Ethnic identity as performance: lessons from Namaqualand', paper presented at the Ethnicity, Identity and Nationalism in South Africa Conference, 20–24 April, Grahamstown, South Africa.

Shoup, J. (1987) *Transhumant Pastoralism in Lesotho: Case Study of the Koeneng-Mapoteng Ward*. Maseru: Land Conservation and Range Development Project, Division of Range Management, Ministry of Agriculture.

Spiegel, A. (1979) 'Migrant labour remittances, the developmental cycle and rural differentiation in a Lesotho community', MA thesis, University of Cape Town.

Staples, R. and Hudson, W. (1938) *An Ecological survey of the mountain areas of Basutoland*, Letchworth: Garden Press.

Starfield, A. and Bleloch, A. (1991) *Building Models for Conservation and Wildlife Management*, Edina: Burgess.

Stein, L. (1992) 'Creative thinking on environment and development', *Democracy in Action, Journal of the Institute for Democratic Alternatives in South Africa*, 6(5): 25.

Strathern, M. (1987) 'Out of context, the persuasive fictions of anthropology', *Current Anthropology*, 28(3): 251–79.

Wilmsen, E. (1989) *Land without Flies: A Political Economy of the Kalahari*, Chicago: University of Chicago Press.

Wilmsen, E. and Denbow, J. (1990) 'Paradigmatic history of San-speaking peoples and current attempts at revision', *Current Anthropology*, 31(5): 489–524.

Zimbabwe Trust (1990) *People, Wildlife and Natural Resources – the CAMPFIRE Approach to Rural Development in Zimbabwe*, Harare: The Zimbabwe Trust.

Chapter 6

Anthropology and the contemporary construction of ethnicity in Indonesia and Britain

C. W. Watson

The future of Europe cannot be founded on the distribution of power or on some new arrangement of the political map which would be based on ethnic divisions. This could not be carried out without large amounts of injustice. As there was (or in some cases hopefully will be) a separation of the State and the Church, there also ought to be a separation of ethnic, national, cultural and language traditions from political arrangements in Europe. Diverse types of political systems and diverse loyalties must learn to live alongside each other. They should not demand political privileges that impinge on the rights of others whether individuals or minorities.

(Ladislav Hejdánek, *Times Higher Educational Supplement*, 29 May 1991)

Nationality doesn't identify 'our side'.
Muses are international, and mine is a Lady
Who speaks all sorts of languages (in translation),
Collects guidebooks, maps, timetables, menus,
Wine lists, and other hedonistic souvenirs.
So what if you were English? I speak that language,
But not its nationality; I love your poetry,
And our imaginary talks – I mean, remembering them –
Please me as proof of how imagination outwits
Half-witted strictures of 'national identity'.

(from Douglas Dunn, 'Audenesques for 1960', *Times Literary Supplement*, 31 July 1992)

As anthropologists we know next to nothing about the countries of the British Isles (with the singular exception, perhaps, of rural Ireland), and I fear that because we therefore underestimate their cultural variety we may be inclined to defend ourselves by saying that there is really not much to know. If anthropology cannot enlighten the complexities of its own national contexts, then it is impotent and trivial.

(Anthony P. Cohen, *Belonging: Identity and Social Organisation in British Rural Cultures*, p. 16)

It is an anthropological commonplace that a sense of group belonging – and ethnicity is of course simply one form of group belonging – is articulated and realised only at junctures of confrontation with those whom one wants to distinguish as others, outsiders to one's own group. The reasons why it is felt necessary to make such distinctions are well known. They range from reasons of marriage rules via issues of territoriality and religion right through to questions of access to economic resources and political power, and anthropologists have always been very good at supplying that fine empirical detail which contextualises the arenas of confrontation.

Anthropologists have also traditionally excelled at showing the precise way in which, at the point of differentiation, ethnicity is articulated: the way in which, for example, members of an ethnic group appeal to the constituent features of a culture, not the least of which is language, but among which are also included modes of dress and diet, institutions of religion and education and styles of political and economic organisation, all of which, taken together, are held to constitute a specific and unique way of life which, particularly when there appears to be a threat to its existence, needs to be preserved and championed: through careful definition and then through planned strategy of active engagement. In addition, anthropologists have learned about ethnicity in recent years from historians and political scientists, or perhaps they have not so much learned anew as rediscovered some of their earlier insights through the exemplary use to which they have been put by historians and political scientists.

From historians, for example, they have taken up the idea of the 'invention of tradition' and shown how in the construction of ethnic identities, groups manufacture, for whatever purpose, historical traditions which demonstrate a continuity between past glory and present aspirations. And indeed anthropologists have also, with a certain shuffling uneasiness, taken the demonstration a further stage by producing examples of the way in which an anthropologist's interpretation of social organisation of a society can, within a generation, be reintroduced into that society, and, in a reified form come to constitute an essential feature of its sense of identity: the anecdote of the informant retiring to the back of the hut to consult the monograph in a foreign language published in a foreign country is all too familiar. Certainly, then, anthropologists are aware of the uses and abuses of history and culture in the construction of ethnicity and their own part in the manufacturing process. If, as Eric Hobsbawm writes (1992: 23), history is to nationalism what the poppy-grower is to the heroin addict, then one might add that the anthropologist is to ethnicity what the analytical chemist is to that same heroin addict, a guarantor of authenticity to whom samples are brought for testing, if there is ever a question of the quality of the goods supplied.

As far as borrowings from political science are concerned, Ben Anderson's notion of 'imagined societies' using several examples from the country and cultures of Indonesia has proved quite seminal in persuading anthropologists to look once more at the anthropological literature on utopias, symbolic communities, voices of prophecy and notions of the millennium, and the way in which elements from these discourses contribute to a nationalism which is inseparable in a colonial, and, one should stress, a post-colonial world, from a political programme (Hobsbawm 1992: 23). And again with that penchant for probing into the minutiae, the anthropologist – who seems here to reveal his or her common ancestry with the archaeologist's absorbed exploration of the intellectual middens of a culture – in excavations of the discourse has skilfully demonstrated the structural and epistemo-logical links between imagination, reality and statement.

To a certain extent, however, we must concede that what I have just described represents accomplishments in relation to a past state of affairs, and that with respect to contemporary matters the present seems almost to have overtaken the anthropologist by stealth. It is not that we are unaware that times have changed in the last three decades – development and modernisation have, after all, for some time been incorporated within the remit of anthropology. Nor is it that we have been loathe to turn our gaze in upon ourselves and our societies. I do not want to argue, then, that anthropology has not changed and developed in relation to the demands of an ethnography of the present. In relation to ethnicity, however, there has been a tendency, perhaps, for anthropology to rest upon its laurels, or the laurels of other disciplines, rather than follow through those important earlier studies of the phenomenon. It is almost as though the present global crises have taken us unawares and we have nothing to say. If anyone should have been able to predict what could happen, it should have been us. Perhaps predictions were made, and I do not know of them, but certainly no one would deny that most of us were caught by surprise. Not surprised by the violence, bloodshed and horror of the confrontations, since, God knows, many of us have seen or know about such things from the countries which we have studied, but that these things could be happening in Europe and that ethnicity and nationalism could be so powerfully yoked together, where we thought the problems of ethnicity, race and multiculturalism, difficult as they were, were of a different dimension – at least as we looked at them from Britain, France, Germany.

The general failure has, I think, lain in the reluctance or inability to make connections: between that sense of local identity, which we are so good at plotting and mapping, and the construction of new national identities with which we are not so familiar and the description of which we leave to others. It is precisely at this point, however, where the local articulates into the national, I suggest, that modern notions of ethnicity are realised, and anthropologists who avoid examining those points of juncture risk getting it drastically wrong. Whereas limited communications in the past, up until thirty years ago say, meant that it was still possible, or at least heuristically acceptable, to bracket out state–community relations in discussion of perceived identities, that is no longer the case: the widespread availability of television, telephone communication and national newspapers compel a recognition that the sites at which a sense of identity is being created are fundamentally different from those which anthropologists have previously analysed (but cf. Skinner 1959).

Although I say there has been a general failure on our part to devote attention to this nodal point of ideological intersection – a failure perhaps all the more surprising because Marxist anthropologists have been pointing us in this direction with respect to local and global economies for some time – there have been some notable exceptions, and indeed these have provided much of the inspiration for this chapter. Robert J. Foster's careful review of the state of the art entitled 'Making National Cultures in the Global Ecumene' (1991), besides admirably drawing together a range of references has, it seems to me, struck exactly the right note in seizing upon the way local and national cultures bear upon each other. And Bruce Kapferer, one of the writers whom Foster refers to at length, has in his book (1988) tried to compare ethnic identities in Sri Lanka and Australia first, by leaning on Dumont and identifying the way in which an ontology (an ideological view of being) becomes in both the Australian and the Sri Lankan cases the well-spring of a sense of ethnic identity. This is demonstrated by arguing, through reference to wide-ranging material – religious, historical, sociological, anecdotal – that notions of egalitarianism and hierarchy separately inform Australian and Sri Lankan identities. And finally, to bring things closer to home – Europe, I mean – Anthony Cohen's edited volume *Belonging*, takes issue with the assumption that in British society, and by implication in all European societies, a sense of local belonging is only a secondary feature in the forms of social organisation in which one participates, and argues strongly that the sense of belonging is, on the contrary, of primary importance, and that we must examine it in all its dense complexity over a range of domains if we are ever to understand that set of references by means of which personal identities are created.

What all these studies have in common is a very acute sense of contemporary reality, a reality which is not the ethnographic present of English prose, not the gnomic tense which pickles in aspic and while subjecting an issue to academic gaze effectively removes it from engaged discussion. Working in a very different stylistic mode which tries hard, it seems to me, to implicate the reader and make of him or her equally a subject through a self-recognition in the texts, these writers all encourage an engagement in debate rather than a simple passing of judgement.

This chapter, similarly, is an attempt to engage anthropology in debating and constructing the present. In briefly comparing the way in which ethnic identities are created in contemporary Indonesia and Britain, my aim is to endorse the proposal that we should look closely at those crucuial junctures at which the local articulates with the national. It seems to me that the similarity of process which we encounter in two very dissimilar countries, reflects not only similar systemic operations by which local and national identities are brought into a relationship, but also that, appearances of difference notwithstanding, it reflects more general, universal, modes of political action.

THE CONSTRUCTION OF ETHNIC IDENTITY IN INDONESIA

Hobsbawm quotes Massimo d'Azeglio as saying after the political unification of Italy: 'We have made Italy, now we have to make Italians.' *Mutatis mutandis* the same could have been said by Indonesian statesmen in 1950 after the unification of Indonesia. The nationalist movement from the mid-1920s had created almost *ex nihilo* a sense of Indonesian identity where previously there existed at the most inclusive level only a regional identity: Javanese, Bugis, Minangkabau, and so on. This notion of region was loosely associated with territory, and more clearly linked with language, but it was most closely identified with what was known as local *adat*. This was a concept which encompassed culture, a way of life, distinctive legal systems and much else, and which by 1920 had been suitably defined and described by Dutch legal scholars to the point of ready adoption by regional groups and representatives as a useful word with which to refer to a distinct sense of ethnic identity. Thus by 1920 there was a constant reference to, for exmaple, *adat Sunda*, *adat Minangkabau*, *adat Ambon*, a terminology still very much in force today.

By 1920, then, there had been a sufficient dissemination of knowledge about regional variety throughout the Indonesia archipelago to provide a repertoire of ethnic reference by which individuals could distinguish themselves from other ethnic groups. Readily available was a profusion of labels by which people recognised the significant ethnic features of others according to such criteria as religion, dress, systems of nomenclature, speech, diet, temperament and behaviour (Skinner 1959).

The élite representatives of these groups coming together in Jakarta in the first two decades of the century perceived very clearly the differences among themselves, but in the political and historical circumstances of the time they realised the need to create a supervening national culture which could be exploited for the purpose of the nationalist programme of achieving independence. Regional identities, then, could quite happily continue to thrive within the regions themselves, but within the nationalist movement, and in those urban associations where people from different ethnic backgrounds were working together, local identities had to be submerged.

Three sociological features facilitated the process of bonding: the first was the common experience of all being subject to Dutch occupation and colonial rule; the second, the availability of a lingua franca, Malay/Indonesian, by then widely spoken throughout the archipelago; the third, the fact that a large majority of the population of the archipelago were Muslims and consequently, at the very least, shared a common set of symbols and associated meanings (for some of the detail here, see Anwar 1980). It was these three features working together within the political struggle of the period 1945–50 which made it possible for people to conceive of themselves as Indonesians, a label which, though it might not at that time have contained much substantive content, made up for lack of cultural substance by being highly politically charged. And it was this political charge which eventually ensured the success of the revolution against the Dutch, since Indonesians were able to convince not only themselves but also influential foreign powers that the idea of an Indonesian nation was a natural and logical extension of political development.

Having achieved independence by persuading people to expunge temporarily all considerations of regional ethnicity while they worked for the common goal of Indonesian nationhood, the government of Indonesia found itself faced with the problem, as I have argued elsewhere (Watson 1987), of transforming a temporary suspension of ethnicity into something more permanent. This required a policy of encouraging people to continue to think in terms of their political identity as being Indonesian, and their cultural identity as regional, but at the same time trying gradually to load notions of Indonesian identity with cultural attributes as some intellectuals had been trying to do with mixed success in the 1930s (Sutherland 1968: 119ff.).

I do not want to discuss the political manoeuvres which kept the sense of being Indonesian on the boil, although I recognise that this political dimension cannot be separated from the cultural in any discussion of Indonesian ethnic identity. My concern here is, rather, with the way in which that sense of cultural, as opposed to political, belonging which in the past was entirely dependent on the institutions of regional *adat*, now began to draw upon new clusters of symbols which had national referents. This shaping of a national culture happened in two ways; first, by the construction of new traditions out of the recent past, particularly the period of the revolution 1945–50, and then by the appropriation of local cultural forms and institutions which were transformed into national institutions, in ways similar to those described by Barth in his general remarks on the activity of political innovators (1969: 35).

In the first place it was again the Indonesian language which became both emblematic of the new traditions and a vehicle for them. Ben Anderson describes very perceptively how this occurred through the incorporation of new terminologies, and the development of a new vocabulary of interpersonal communication which dispensed with the hierarchisation of traditional terms of personal reference; and replaced them with egalitarian forms such as the words *saudara* ('sibling') and *bung* ('comrade brother') (Anderson 1966). As a literary vehicle, the Indonesian of the journals and the fiction of the period consolidated the memories of the revolution, and provided the urban population at least, with a common store of experiences on which they could draw; and the consequent act of sharing, an 'imagined past', as much as any imagined community of the future, united people in a shared belonging. To these informal and indirect operations must be added the programmes of the government specifically designed to give shape to notions of Indonesian identity.

The most well-known of the new national politico-cultural traditions created by the government was *Pancasila*, the set of five principles of State. The origins of *Pancasila*, its development from 1945–85, and the use to which it has been put have been thoroughly discussed, and there is no need to repeat the descriptions here. At the same time as *Pancasila* was being defined and disseminated throughout the archipelago, the government was also working to introduce a uniform administrative service which dissolved the differences which the Dutch had recognised among the various *adat* regions. Equally important were the extension of Indonesian schooling and the rapid promulgation of a nationalist history of Indonesia.

The writing of the nationalist history is in fact an excellent example of the second manner of cultural Indonesianisation: the appropriation and transformation of local cultural traditions and their absorption into a national framework. Heroes and heroines whose names had been celebrated locally as opponents of the Dutch and leaders of their communities were now endowed with new status as *pahlawan nasional*, national heroes, figures like Diponegoro from Java, Tjut Na Din from Aceh, Tuanku Imam Bonjol from Minangkabau, Arun Palakka from Makassar. These names were included in the history books of the nation to be memorised by the new generations of schoolchildren. The ethnic or regional origins of the heroes were known, but they were celebrated as Indonesian heroes *avant la lettre*. The process is of course a familiar one. What is perhaps striking about it in the Indonesian case was the rapidity with which it was done, and the apparent success of the enterprise.

At another level Indonesian culture absorbed regional songs, from Ambon, from the Batak, from the Batavian *kroncong* tradition, which together with the new songs of the revolution, became part of a new popular Indonesian repository. A similar, though not identical trend, developed in relation to dress. Women's regional costumes are very distinctive, but this very distinctiveness could be exploited to advantage in order to exemplify the national motto 'Unity in Diversity' without in any way encouraging the growth of political ethnicity. Thus on certain annual holidays which were national days, most notably *Hari Kartini* ('Women's Day') on 21 April, women were encouraged to wear their regional costumes thereby establishing a ritual fusing of the local and the national. On other occasions, for example, the anniversary of the declaration of independence on 17 August, the uniform national dress – the *kebaya pendek* – was obligatory. In these ways, then, the government could encourage regional pride, indeed make it a positive factor in nation-building, without jeopardising the unity of the state.

However, throughout this period when these moves to build up a store of Indonesian cultural symbols were taking place, at the lowest levels of social organisation within the family, the neighbourhood, the village, there was occurring that primary socialisation, that growth of a sense of intimate belonging, which, as Cohen argues so convincingly (1982: 12ff.), is not determined by wider political and social contexts but determines them or at least determines how those contexts are perceived, interpreted and evaluated by the individual. It is at these lower levels that a knowledge of a way of life is formed in childhood, a knowledge which in later years is used and shaped to select those specific attributes which will be held as critical features of one's own ethnicity. To take an Indonesian example, the Minangkabau child very soon learns how the family and kinship system in which she is growing up operates, and her self-definition is a product of the various statuses she perceives she has within that system as daughter, niece, cross-cousin, grandchild, and so on. That social reality is primary for her. As she grows up, and her experiential horizons widen through direct and indirect contact with other groups, she learns that this system of kinship is distinctive of her own group, and quintessential of her own ethnic identity, perceived from within and without. She may come to value her own matrilineal system negatively, as I have known some Minangkabau to do, but she will always recognise it as fundamentally constitutive of her own belonging to a *suku*, an ethnic group.

The development of an awareness of regional ethnic identity in the 1950s in Indonesia, then, was not so much a reaction to the imposition of a national identity, but the continuation of a trend which had been a function of the economic development of the archipelago from the beginning of the century. The take-up of economic and educational opportunities meant increasing inter-island migration. In the 1950s, students in particular, at upper-secondary and tertiary level, were moving in droves to the large towns of Java, some of which, Bandung and Yogyakarta for example, became student cities. After they graduated, many stayed on to find employment. It was there in these cities above all that strong and vigorous ethnic traditions developed, as indeed one might have expected. Here were sizeable ethnic minorities, financially not very well off, pooling their economic and psychological resources by living together in regional hostels, forming regional associations and developing a sense of corporate identity which relied heavily on a set of symbols of ethnicity (Bruner 1974).

At one level symbols were relatively superficial in their significance, recognisable badges of identity, about which jokes could be made with relative impunity, dress, songs, food, for example. At another level, however, ethnic characteristics were treated more solemnly when it was a question of attitudes to religion, moral values, temperament, language, notions of friendship. These cities, then, were the ideal environment in which ethnicity could thrive and ethnic stereotypes quickly develop into instant judgements of other cultures. The distinctive features of the Javanese, the Sundanese, the Minangkabau, the Bugis, the Batak, the Acehnese and the Chinese, were all summarily encoded into types, though, interestingly, all the ascribed characteristics referred, by and large, to male stereotypes.

This growth of regional pride and ethnic commitment occasionally clashed with the national ideology of unity. There were occasional interethnic student clashes, and when regional rebellions occurred in the 1950s, loyalties were divided between region and state, although few, it is generally acknowledged (Booth 1992: 33, 36), wanted to see the dissolution of the nation into regional fragments. The arena where more worrying trends occurred, was to be found in the competition for economic resources and professional opportunities where the spectre of *sukuisme* ('ethnic bias') loomed large. This was not simply a question of hostility to the Chinese who seemed to have captured exclusive control of the retail trade, although this was part of it, but at a more general level there was dissatisfaction that a kind of nepotism, through extending patronage along networks first of kinship then of the ethnic group, was operating throughout the civil service. Thus, for example, in Bandung the heartland of the Sunda region there was a feeling among non-Sundanese that senior posts in the local administration, in teaching and in higher education were being reserved for ethnic Sundanese.

This general belief that principles of ethnicity were operating in a discriminatory way was of immediate concern to the representatives of government, both out of a general sense of principle that such behaviour was not consistent with the type of democratic society they were advocating, and because of the latent threat it posed to national unity. (For a fascinating account of the dynamics of this process at a local level see Liddle 1967.) The secular nationalist political parties, the Partai Nasional Indonesia (PNI, Indonesian National Party) and the

Partai Komunis Indonesia (PKI, Indonesian Communist Party) too, also denounced *sukuisme*, again both out of reasons of principle and because they recognised that *sukuisme* was one of the features which were employed in recruitment to religious parties whose followers were often identified by regional blocs. However, even these secular parties could not escape the effects of different ethnic perceptions and values in relation to party policy. Ruth McVey has shown in a fascinating article (1986) how, within the PKI, divisions along ethnic lines emerged in relation to the appropriateness of using Javanese mythical symbology as a vehicle for Communist ideas.

There existed, then, a dynamic tension in the relationship between the claims of nationalism and ethnicity. Sometimes these claims were not in competition, and for the individual the circumstances of the occasion very clearly dictated whether an ethnic or nationalist response was required. Again this is much as we would be led to believe by theory. In the context of the Bandung Conference of Asian and African nations in 1955, counting oneself an Indonesian was a matter of pride, as it was eight years later in the period of confrontation with Malaysia. On the other hand, admissions policies in universities which seemed to favour students from one ethnic group over another engendered resentment and evoked a sense of ethnic loyalty. But this latter example brings out the different levels at which nationalist and ethnic consciousness operate. Nationalism is called upon at times of crisis and special occasion and is only sporadically brought to the individual's consciousness – during times of war, political conferences, sporting occasions, annual remembrance parades – whereas ethnicity is constantly present, much closer to the bone, much quicker to realise itself in everyday experience in domestic and professional contexts. Although the comparison is perhaps just a little bit too neat, one could argue that the tension lies in balancing the needs of being a citizen and being an individual, the public and the personal self, a duty to an ideal concept of the national good and a duty to the immediate needs of one's loved ones.

If it was issues such as these which shaped an individual's sense of self in Indonesia in the 1950s and early 1960s soon after the creation of the nation, how does the present situation compare, and in what forms does anthropology in particular, perceive the continuing realisation of tensions of identity? Rather than attempt to answer the question macroscopically I want to approach the analysis in the way anthropologists have traditionally found fruitful, from observation of the small community, in this case Kerinci in central Sumatra.

ETHNICITY AND NATIONALISM IN THE 1990s: THE VIEW FROM THE INDONESIAN VILLAGE

Two brief recollections of fieldwork experience can perhaps serve to summarise recent developments of national and ethnic consciousness. The first is of a small boy aged about 5 brought to me proudly by his father. 'Look at this', his father said to me. 'Now, 'Mun, come on, let's have it, *Pancasila*, and there's a hundred rupiah for you.' 'Mun stood upright and began to chant in a strong voice 'Pancasila. Satu. Ketuhanan Yang Maha Esa, Dua . . .' until he had repeated the five principles of state philosophy word perfect. His father beamed and gave 'Mun Rp. 100 and I, too, smiled, congratulated him and gave him Rp. 100. The second incident occurred while watching television in the mid-1980s in Kerinci. Television was a relatively new phenomenon having only arrived there in 1979. As a family we were about to watch a weekly cultural programme. When the programme was announced, we learned it was to be a presentation of a Javanese *wayang* programme. The family turned from it in disappointment and the father of the family said, critically, 'I don't know why they show all these Javanese programmes. They're not Indonesian, they're Javanese. Why don't they put on something which everyone can understand.' He went off into another room and the others too drifted off after a matter of minutes leaving the programme without an audience.

What the first experience brought home was the way in which *Pancasila* was coming to be universally accepted as a symbol for Indonesian-ness. Again much has been written about this in recent years in relation to the political manoeuvres of the Government in the last fifteen years, and the details of the formal campaign both to instil a knowledge of *Pancasila*, and its antecedents and consequences through mass in-service training programmes as well as through politically imposing it as the sole fundamental principle (*asas tunggal*) of all associations, are now well documented (Watson 1987). The procedures here have simply built upon and developed the strategy of the 1950s. The fact that the boy and his father took such pride in the ability to recite the *Pancasila* shows the degree to which *Pancasila* and, implicitly, a commitment to Indonesian-ness had become so central to the consciousness of Indonesians even in relatively remote societies. Political and religious associations at the time were challenging the requirement to make *Pancasila* the fundamental principle of their organisation, but as far as ordinary Indonesians throughout the archipelago are concerned *Pancasila* not only reflects and symbolises their sense of Indonesian-ness but also contains a moral philosophy which they endorse.

To be Indonesian, however, is one thing, to be Javanese, another, and the television watcher expressing his irritation at the *wayang* was voicing a commonly heard complaint about the stridency with which Javanese ethnicity appears now to be promoted. We should perhaps leave politics to one side here, though at the same time noting the word *Javanisasi* ('Javanisation') referring to the bureaucratic control of the centre and to the increasing presence of Javanese civil servants in important official positions in the outer islands has taken on strong pejorative connotations. The protest is, however, not confined to the domain of politics, but at a more general level refers to the way Java is, by the Javanese, thought to represent Indonesia: Javanese attitudes, Javanese values, a Javanese culture of bureaucracy, even Javanese linguistic usage, seem to other Indonesians to be increasingly conspicuous. Javanese culture and any other culture within Indonesia is all very well in its place, but it must always be recognised as simply one part of a much larger unit, not as a *pars pro toto*, not synecdochically representing Indonesia.

Within Kerinci, then, perceptions of other cultures still conform to the stereotypes established in the 1950s. Communications infrastructures now link Kerinci very quickly and easily to Jakarta and Java; there is a great deal of travelling not only by students but by families, and there is much more exposure to other ethnic groups. Furthermore, there is considerable in-migration to Kerinci and the central market area contains a great variety of people. The stereotypes provide a quick and convenient way of understanding and engaging with others: the Javanese official, the Batak forestry specialist, the Minangkabau pedlar, the Sundanese policeman, all require different approaches if one is to deal with them successfully.

However, at the same time as recognising the specific characteristic of other ethnic groups, in Kerinci at least, there appears to be uncertainty about defining what constitutes a Kerinci identity. This is not through lack of trying. While never wanting the Javanese part to be taken as a whole, the Kerinci people none the less appreciate the mosaic effect of ethnic contributions to the nation and see the value of their own culture being recognised as a contributory part. The last twenty years has seen revival of Kerinci dances and Kerinci songs, the devising of Kerinci costumes, in short the invention of traditions. And again the anthropologist has been asked to play this part as guarantor and demonstrator that Kerinci *adat* is unique, that it differs from that of its neighbours in Jambi and Minangkabau, that it has regional heroes of national status and that it played a part in national history (Watson 1984).

In relation to these visible phenomena there is a notion of Kerinci identity, but these are not the elements by which an individual feels him- or herself to be constituted: they are external to that individual and their presence or absence, however much a matter of concern to individuals, are not of fundamental importance to a sense of self. Outside Kerinci itself, in Jakarta among the Kerinci people permanently settled, the newly invented traditions are important as a stock of cultural items to which they can appeal when asked by non-Kerinci to define their culture – compare the situation among the Gayo in Jakarta described by Bowen (1991: 258). Among themselves, however, precisely because there is a perception of the artificiality of it all, these inventions are taken only half seriously. The major areas in which ethnicity plays a role are still drawn from the everyday areas of domestic and professional affaires.

Those regional and subregional organisations set up in the 1950s as student welfare societies, have now expanded and taken on a greater variety of roles. The Kerinci organisation in Jakarta regularly brings people together on the occasions of *rites de passage* and in times of crisis. A network exists for communication and the exchange of information, and this network comprehensively encompasses all ethnic Kerinci from different walks of life, of different ages and of different social statuses. It is very much their ethnic identity which brings them together and makes them conscious not only of their origins but their continuing commitment to each other and to something which they recognise as the common good of Kerinci. A gathering of Kerinci people constitutes an environment in which they can be most immediately at home, made up as it is of those with whom they grew up and associated in their extended families, their villages and the schools they attended in Kerinci. Furthermore, not only does the existence of the organisation reflect a sense of obligation and commitment of its members to one another, there is also a sense of corporate responsibility towards what is happening in Kerinci. Thus there are discussions about the election of the new *bupati* (village head), the administrative head of the Kerinci region, and whether corporately they should try to bend the ear of the governor to favour a particular candidate, or about some proposed development plan and its advisability. One especially concrete form which this sense of corporate commitment has taken recently was the return to Kerinci from Jakarta,

Padang and Jambi in June 1991 of senior Kerinci intellectuals and businessmen on the occasion of a ritual feast (*kenduri sko*) at the request of the *bupati* to discuss the strategies for the future development of Kerinci. It is through such organisations as these, more than through the ostensibly 'cultural' manifestations that Kerinci ethnicity, and, by extension, other regional identities in Indonesia are most effectively realised.

In sum, then, observing the Indonesian experience of the past forty years it is reasonable to conclude that nationalism and ethnicity on the whole co-exist in creative tension. Commitment to the nation does not lead to the dissolution of commitment to ethnicity and regionalism: the two operate at different levels, and it is only when there is a danger of the confusion of the two – when Java is taken for the nation – that the tension might become explosive. The gradual loading of the notion of Indonesian identity with cultural ballast has not occurred at the expense of ethnic identity, but complements it, and indeed valorises local ethnic traditions. By comparison, then, let us now turn to British society to see whether a similar analysis can help us to understand manifestations of nationalism and ethnicity there.

NATIONALISM AND ETHNICITY IN BRITAIN

In the late 1940s and early 1950s Britain, too, was recovering from the aftermath of war. The immediate problems were to develop the economy and the fulfilment of the people's expectations that a new more egalitarian British society was about to be ushered in. The development of the economy took longer than anticipated, and much of the goodwill and tolerance of the country towards the efforts of the government had evaporated in the early 1950s. To restore confidence and maintain a sense of corporate endeavour, an attempt was made to exploit the symbols of nationalism in a manner continuous with, but slightly different from, the rallying of the nation in the war years. If in the war the appeal had been to the 'bulldog spirit' and 'true British grit' and to slogans like 'Britain can take it', the new appeal to nationalism played upon a sense of corporate pride in Britain's institutions and accomplishments.

This notion of Britishness was in fact inseparable from Englishness. The English have always been the Javanese of Britain, and indeed one can argue that during the 1950s that English colonisation of Britain had led not only to English symbols and English culture dominating the new nationalism but to implicit suppression of regional ethnicity. The process of Anglicisation of British nationalism was not a new one. Unlike many of the nations of mainland Europe – France, Germany, Italy, which had, it is often argued, only acquired a true sense of nationhood in the nineteenth century – Britain or rather England, through a variety of circumstances had passed through a stage of creating a national symbolic heritage dating back at least to the Elizabethan period. Whenever the necessity arose, therefore, these national symbols could be dusted off, polished and brought out for public display at a moment's notice, or, to change the metaphor, those symbols could be reinterpreted and reinvigorated and used in new sets and combinations suggesting continuity, while in fact being put to fresh purpose. Hugh Cunningham describes this process very illuminatingly in his account of the development over the centuries of the language of patriotism which relied on a discourse of what constituted English traditions and values of freedom and democracy (Cunningham 1989).

There was, then, in the 1950s a ready-made set of symbols, mottoes and slogans waiting to be reappropriated and turned to good national use. The quintessential institutions, the monarchy, the Commonwealth – still the Empire in many people's eyes – and Westminster were intact, and it was a fairly simple matter to create the illusion of grandeur once more. The Festival of Britain in 1951 was designed to do principally that, celebrate Britain's position in the world, not as the most powerful nation, but as the most accomplished and – in the people's own eyes – the most civilised. The Coronation of Queen Elizabeth in 1953 built very successfully on this new nationalism by astutely evoking continuity and tradition through comparisons between the two Elizabeths and the triumphant ages which they both represented. Reference to a new Elizabethan age, to a new dawning of British culture in the theatre and the cinema were all designed to stir the nation. (As a boy I can remember being given for Christmas a subscription to a new journal entitled the *Young Elizabethan* in which all these triumphs of the new age were described and applauded.) And sport, too, began to loom very large as emblematic of the nation as a whole, not simply a side-show for cricket buffs. Everest was conquered, Bannister broke the four-minute mile. In popular culture, the old enemies, the Germans, were still being defeated each week in the cinema and in comics such *Hotspur* and *Rover* which circulated among schoolchildren; and for adults, paperback war novels massaged British self-esteem. A sense of 'Bliss it was in that dawn to be alive', a strong confidence in the nation and a tremendous feeling of national self-righteousness were in the air.

Of course these emotions and self-assessment could not be

sustained. Suez and national humiliation were just around the corner; and race riots in the streets, the movement of the colonies towards independence, and then trouble in Ireland, very quickly spelled an end to the spurious buoyancy of the mid-1950s, leaving only, it could be argued, the achievement of personal economic gain as a spur to national development. It was, however, not only these external events which pricked the bubble of complacency; rather, I want to argue, it was a structural flaw at a much deeper level: at those junctures where the cultures of nationalism, ethnicity and class meet.

The reason for the collapse of British nationalism in the 1950s is to be found in its lack of representativeness, both in terms of its failure to devise substantial rather than simply colourful symbols of national values, and in terms of its failure to give recognition to the specific virtues of cultures and classes other than the middle class of the English south. In other words there was no concerted attempt to create a British culture, either at a government level – where the promulgation of a *Pancasila* might have been impossible, but where some sense of civic pride and direct participation in national institutions could have been instilled – or at the level of incorporating from the regions or from the variety of ethnic minorities, cultural features which could be integrated into a national self-image. Instead, what occurred was the swamping of Britain by one particular regional culture, as though Indonesia were to be taken over not simply by general Javanese cultural values, but by the norms of the *kraton* (the Sultan's palace) of Solo.

The way of life held up for emulation in the press, in the cinema and on television, and in the schools, as well as in the popular books and leisure pursuits, whether this was in terms of correct speech, styles of dress and eating, matters of etiquette, church-going, or social attitudes, represented the norms of one small but powerful section in the country. Differences from these norms were regarded as deviations, and those who had been brought up in different social environments were forced to learn, as they entered into adult life, new Southern ways of speech, new ways of dressing, new styles of social intercourse. The models were there on the screen; there were books of etiquette that could be bought and studied; and even children could from an early age be unconsciously and painlessly inducted into an assimilation of this Southern or Home Counties middle-class way of seeing things. (In this respect Frank Boyce has a fascinating article describing through an examination of a series of children's books, how it was indeed ways of seeing which were controlled (1989).) As others have often observed, it was an attempt to turn the clock back, to proceed with that process of

Anglicisation which had been marked out in the 1920s and 1930s, as though nothing had happened. And ultimately it could not last because the assumptions of class differentiation upon which those national images depended had been abandoned and rejected during the war, and were no longer acceptable. The genteel suppression of regional, ethnic and class difference, having once been exposed for what it was, could never again masquerade as an authentic source of nationalism.

An account of the rediscovery of ethnicity and regionalism – it is sometimes difficult to distinguish between the two – in Britain during the 1960s is beyond the scope of this chapter, but it is important to note briefly what those manifestations of ethnicity were, and how they impinged upon and affected nationalism. Globally, perhaps the most widely known of the regional identities to come to the fore was, thanks to the Beatles, that of Liverpool. The accent, once regarded as funny and as deviant as the other regional accents, now began to acquire prestige. People began to imitate it, and individual personalities on radio and television began to use it unashamedly. This had a snowball effect and consequently other regional accents were 'discovered' and given due recognition. The BBC in its turn abandoned its policy of trying to impose Received Pronunciation on the population of the country and accepted regional variation. The attention given to accent, however, was simply part of a far broader and deeper growing interest in regionalism and a desire at the local level of people to see their traditions, culture and history celebrated nationally – a desire identical to the peoples of the Indonesian regions wanting to see their traditions celebrated nationally. To cater to that demand – in addition to the boosting of regional television and radio networks – regionally focused television programmes were devised for national transmission, sit-coms, drama series, documentaries, bringing home to people throughout the country, particularly to those in the south, that there were several versions of what it meant to be British.

The pressures to conform to Home Counties norms did not disappear overnight. (As an instance of this, I remember as late as 1970 hearing one Oxford graduate say of a mutual friend who had just graduated with a first in history from Balliol that it was a pity he spoke with a regional accent since his chances of social advancement would inevitably be limited.) But at least there was a new tolerance of variation which seemed to hold out a promise for the future. There were, however, contrary trends emerging at the same time in relation to new immigrant communities, which gave cause for uneasiness.

In exactly the same manner in which a uniform and homogeneous

British culture had been foisted on the indigenous inhabitants in the 1950s, so, at the end of the decade and through the 1960s and 1970s, the same procedures were employed in relation to immigrant minorities who were being compelled to subscribe to notions of Britishness which were equally partial and limited. A consequence of this was the development of a spurious 'us and them' dichotomy, encouraged by irresponsible politicians and indirectly supported by the media and the educational establishment. The irony of the situation was that the developments of the 1960s had shown 'us' that there was no such homogeneous community, that we spoke with different accents, held different things sacred, celebrated different traditions and saw life from different perspectives which had been determined by the region, class and educational background we came from and – but this only became clear in the 1970s – by our gender. Similarly, we should have seen that 'them' was not a homogeneous group of people, and the darkness of skin was not indicative of a common sharing of cultural attributes. The consensus, however, appeared to be that whereas regionalism – which was what we had already – was acceptable, and to be encouraged for the colour and variety it added to natural life, ethnicity – which was being brought in by outsiders – was suspect and to be suppressed.

Comparing Britain and Indonesia at the beginning of the 1960s we can, then, identify how despite the very different cultural, historical and political antecedents in both countries, similar pressures were affecting a sense of unity in the two nations. In both cases the importance of creating a commitment to national political and economic goals was recognised, and the first step in engendering that commitment was the reinforcing of a sense of common identity. Indonesia, a young country, needed to establish a set of traditions and cultural symbols *a novo*; Britain, on the other hand, could exploit those traditions built up over three centuries. Indonesia, while recognising the importance of a new national identity, very early on also recognised that regional cultures needed to be given national credit. Britain, on the other hand, having been too complacent in its reliance on out-of-date national symbols had attempted to suppress regionalism, but had been compelled to reassess the value of cultural difference to the common good in the 1960s.

At the end of the 1980s in Indonesia, although observers could not fail to note the rumblings of regional discontent both in relation to an equitable distribution of economic resources and, in Aceh and Irian Jaya in particular, with respect to political autonomy as demanded by separatist groups, none the less, the overall balance between ethnicity and nationalism, as we have seen, appeared to be more or less acceptable. The only major worrying issue to arise in this respect lay in perceptions of the increasing Javanisation of the archipelago, some-thing of which the central government seemed unaware. There had been, then, over the course of thirty years a series of shifts and alignments with respect to perceptions of ethnicity and nationalism. To what extent had comparable shifts in perception occurred in British society?

NATIONALISM AND ETHNICITY IN THE NINETIES: THE VIEW FROM THE ENGLISH VILLAGE

Two focal points of community life in Britain today are the local primary school and the post office, and, consequently, it is particularly appropriate that my two illustrative anecdotes are drawn from those two locations.

At a meeting of the governing board of the local primary school near where I live in east Kent there was recently some discussion about whether the governors should agree to the circulation of a government questionnaire to the parents of schoolchildren which requested information in relation to ethnicity: the ethnic origins of parents, religion, first language spoken at home, and so on. There was strong resistance on the part of some governors to the circulation, the argument being that the questionnaire was an intrusion on privacy. When it was pointed out that the collection of such information might assist in the teaching of children from non-WASP backgrounds, one of the responses was that the school always had done and always would treat everyone equally, and that there was no question of discriminating against a pupil on grounds of colour or creed: a classic statement of 'colour blindness' from the heartland of white, south, middle-class England.

The post-office story is simply an overheard remark. A few years ago the then owners of the local post office were about to retire. They had just requested permission to develop some land at the back of their property from the local county council and permission had been refused. Maggie – not her real name – was apparently incensed by the council's attitude, and, according to the overheard remark, she had said that she was now 'going to sell the post office to the first Pakistani buyer she could find and to hell with the council'. The implication was that she no longer cared about the quality of village life and that if a Pakistani family moved in and things changed, that was not her concern. Eventually the post office did change hands, and a South

Asian family moved in, not Pakistanis but Sikhs from India, but still Pakistanis to most of their white customers. In fact they have settled in well and now are properly integrated into village life.

The governors' debate shows how issues of ethnicity are at last beginning to impinge on the general consciousness of people at large, even in areas with no migrant communities. Of course, over the last ten years or so, a number of spectacular media issues such as the resignation of a headmaster in Bradford over policy issues associated with questions of race, and the *Satanic Verses* affair have alerted people to the existence of ethnic-minority concerns but the real nature of the culture of ethnic minorioties has never been properly understood. It is true, however, that in response to the same pressures which forced a recognition of regional values in the 1960s, there is now a greater awareness of the special needs of ethnic minorities: television programmes in minority languages, black television presenters, the establishment of a Commission for Racial Equality, the generation of more images of black British culture, the coining of the term Black British itself. All these are welcome moves in the right direction, although there is still a long way to go and some of the steps taken seem little more than tokenism.

If one is correct in arguing that the government has been insufficiently interventionist in promoting a tolerance and under-standing of ethnic-minority cultures, and that the positive changes in public awareness which have occurred are the product of pressure from below, one can also argue that in a contrary fashion the government has been overinterventionist in relation to nationalism, but the details of the argument are complex.

I have been implying in relation to Indonesia that, despite my initial scepticism, the promotion of national values through the promulgation of *Pancasila* succeeded in creating a sense of civic pride and genuine national commitment, and that the legacy of that nationalism born out of the struggle for independence had been fruitfully used to the common good, creating an admirable sense of corporate solidarity and mutual responsibility supported by, rather than militating against, networks of ethnic and regional loyalties. Why should I find the same endeavours on the part of the British State to promote a nationalist spirit suspect?

A partial answer must be in the well-known image of the Janus-face of British nationalism much discussed in New Left circles in Britain. One of the faces of nationalism is universally acceptable, and both the Left and the Right protest when the other tries to claim a monopoly over British patriotism. The ideologues from Orwell to Michael Foot and even Eric Hobsbawm (Barnett 1989: 147) see a virtue in promoting, disseminating and teaching British values and extolling patriotism. To that extent there is an endorsement of the government's recent attempts to reorganise the educational system of the country to ensure that there is an appropriate transmission of values, a real understanding of a way of life. Where the argument begins, and where critics identify the unacceptable face of Janus, is in the vehicles employed for the transmission of those values. The debates turn on whether, for example, the emphasis on learning the dates of great British victories do much either for a real appreciation of historical process or for the spirit of international understanding. The consequence is more likely to be, as it must be noted we find in Indonesia, chauvinism and xenophobia, of the kind which surfaced during the Falklands War and now threatens to wreck the Maastricht Treaty.

The danger of this ill-defined, narrow version of nationalism is that it creates a ground swell of enthusiasm for an empty concept. The 'British way of life' which my fellow villagers in the south of England see threatened by an Indian family moving into the community is a notion which most of them would find hard to define. On the other hand, again by one of those quirks of irony, it appears to be something which the new immigrant communities are very much aware of.

As in the Indonesian case, where ethnic groups in Jakarta create associations of mutual support which enable individuals to maintain an easy balance between ethnic and national identities, so, too, in British cities ethnic minorities operate in the same way, celebrating their origins yet simultaneously appreciative of a national life style, which despite its limitations provides opportunities, upholds basic freedoms, and strives for equality and justice. At a superficial level they may support the cricket team of their country of origin in Test series, but in discussions with their cousins who still remain in India, Pakistan or the Caribbean they are in no doubt about differences in national life style and their loyalty to a British way of life.

In the village of the south of England, then, as in the villages of Kerinci, there is uncertainty about the constitution of an ethnic identity which all feel they possess, which is to be found, if nowhere else, in the maintenance of a 'way of life', potentially threatened by outsiders. Where that ethnic identity is more clearly definable is in urban contexts where ethnicity and an implicit commitment to national ideals coexist. The difference, however, between a Kerinci and a Kentish villager's perception of their everyday cultures is that for the people of Kent there is no real appreciation of the fact that their way of life is but one of many in British society, whereas the Kerinci villagers know their limitations.

CONCLUSION

An anthropological approach to questions of ethnicity must always begin with people's perceptions of their own identity in relation to others, but beyond that lies the task of reconstructing the genesis of those perceptions. The complex political and technological developments which have occurred in the past thirty years have inevitably altered the manner in which those perceptions have come into being by the sudden juxtaposing of ideas of self and community, derived from primary socialisation, with concepts of exogenous origin carried by the vehicles of the new technologies. Anthropologists observing the making of the present should be prepared to document the perceptions which arise from these juxtapositions and the behaviour to which they give rise.

In comparing British and Indonesian societies I have argued that perceived national needs, in particular the universal need to create a just and prosperous society, have demanded in both cases strategies for harnessing the forces of nationalism and ethnicity for the common good. In Indonesia this led from a very early stage in the nation's history to a sustained attempt to create a national culture with a universally accepted set of values. However, when simultaneous with this construction of a national culture, a spontaneous movement from within regional cultures reinforced a sense of ethnic identity, the latter far from being suppressed was encouraged, within limits, and ultimately came to underpin the state's philosophy of 'unity in diversity'. Recently, however, the major ethnic group, the Javanese, in the perceptions of some appear to have arrogated to themselves the on-going creation of Indonesian tradition.

In Britain, by contrast, the task of the last thirty years has been to dismantle a construction of British national identity which had already become too closely identified with a class and a region. This, too, meant an empowerment of regional and ethnic identities, although it did not appear to mean a parallel substantive construction of a new British identity. After thirty years the importance of the latter is recognised, but the task of the construction is beset with pitfalls of which the most difficult is the risk of a slide into narrow chauvinism. Fortunately, there now seems to be some understanding of that principle of recognising and positively evaluating expressions of ethnicity, although from Westminster to the Kentish village there are still a number of people who need to be convinced. In both countries, I suggest, the future of interethnic relations will depend heavily on anthropologists maintaining their vigilance in observing how the present is being constructed.

REFERENCES

Anderson, B.R.O.G. (1966) 'The languages of Indonesian politics', *Indonesia*, 1: 89–116.

Anwar, Kh. (1980) *Indonesian: The Development and Use of a National Language*, Yogyakarta: Gadjah Mada University Press.

Barnett, A. (1989) 'After Nationalism', in R. Samuel (ed.), *Patriotism: The Making and Unmaking of British National Identity*, Volume I, *History and Politics*, London and New York: Routledge, pp. 140–55.

Barth, F. (ed.) (1969) *Ethnic Groups and Boundaries*, London: Allen and Unwin.

Booth, A. (1992) 'Can Indonesia survive as a unitary state?', *Indonesia Circle*, No. 58 (June): 32–47.

Bowen, J. R. (1991) *Sumatran Politics and Poetics: Gayo History, 1890–1898*, New Haven and London: Yale University Press.

Boyce, F. Cottrell (1989) 'I-Spy', in R. Samuel (ed.), *Patriotism: The Making and Unmaking of British National Identity*, Volume II, *Minorities and Outsiders*, London and New York: Routledge, pp. 9–17.

Bruner, E. M. (1974) 'The expression of ethnicity in Indonesia', in A. Cohen (ed.), *Urban Ethnicity*, London: Tavistock, pp. 251–80.

Cohen, A. (ed.) (1974) *Urban Ethnicity*, London: Tavistock.

Cohen, A. P. (ed.) (1982) *Belonging: Identity and Social Organisation in British Rural Cultures*, Manchester: Manchester University Press.

Cunningham, H. (1989) 'The language of patriotism', in R. Samuel (ed.), *Patriotism: The Making and Unmaking of British National Identity*, Volume I, *History and Politics*, London and New York: Routledge, pp. 57–89.

Foster, R. J. (1991) 'Making national cultures in the global ecumene', *Annual Review of Anthropology*, 20: 235–60.

Hobsbawm, E. (1992) 'Whose fault-line is it anyway?', lecture to American Anthropological Association, repr. *Anthropology Today* 8(1): 3–8; and *New Statesman*, 24 April, 1992, pp. 23–6.

Kapferer, B. (1988) *Legends of People, Myths of State: Violence and Political Culture in Sri Lanka and Australia*, Washington, DC and London: Smithsonian Institution Press.

Liddle, W. R. (1967) 'Suku Simalungun, an ethnic group in search of representation', *Indonesia*, 3 (April): 1–28.

McVey, R. T. (1986) 'The Wayang controversy in Indonesian communism', in M. Hobart and R. Taylor (eds), *Context, Meaning and Power in Southeast Asia*, Southeast Asia Programme, Ithaca: Cornell University, pp. 21–5.

Samuel, R. (ed.) (1989) *Patriotism: The Making and Unmaking of British*

National Identity, Volume I, *History and Politics,* Volume II, *Minorities and Outsiders,* London and New York: Routledge.

Skinner, G. W. (ed.) (1959) *Local, Ethnic, and National Loyalties in Village Indonesia: A Symposium,* Yale University Cultural Report Series, Southeast Asia Studies, New York: Institute of Pacific Relations.

Sutherland H. (1968) 'Pudjangga Baru: aspects of Indonesian intellectual life in the 1930s', *Indonesia,* 6: 106–27.

Watson, C. W. (1984) *Kerinci: Two Historical Studies.* Occasional Paper No.3, Centre of South-East Asian Studies, University of Kent at Canterbury.

—— (1987) *State and Society in Indonesia,* Occasional Paper No. 8, Centre of South-East Asian Studies, University of Kent at Canterbury.

Index